<u>Mission</u>:

Christmas

Youth Programs & Ideas for Advent

Bryan Brooks

Abingdon Press
Nashville

Cover design: Keely Moore

05 06 07 08 09 10 11 12 13 14—10 9 8 7 6 5 4 3 2 1

Contents

How to Use

How to Use Mission: Christmas

About
MISSION: CHRISTMAS

Advent is a season of preparation. For four weeks in the late fall and early winter, Christians around the world prepare for Christmas, the day we celebrate God's greatest gift: Jesus Christ, God's Son. Advent prepares you for Christmas; but what prepares you for Advent? How can you make Advent meaningful for your youth?

The purpose of MISSION: CHRISTMAS is to provide youth leaders, Christian education directors, and Sunday school teachers with programs and ideas they can use in a variety of settings throughout the Advent season. This resource will help you prepare lessons and activities that will teach your youth to better understand and observe this sacred time of year.

Programs

Sunday Programs. MISSION: CHRISTMAS contains five programs: one for each of the four Sundays in Advent, and one for the Sunday after Christmas. You can use these programs during the Sunday school hour or as a part of Sunday- or Wednesday-evening youth fellowship.

Each program is based on a New and Old Testament Scripture (from *The Revised Common Lectionary*) and a key question, which is printed

in the center of the opening page of each program. Each Sunday program includes at least six activities related to that program's Scriptures and key question, a one- to two-page article explaining how that Sunday's topic relates to youth and to the Advent season, and an easy-to-use chart that lists the supplies needed for each activity.

Reproducible Pages. At least one reproducible worksheet supplements each Sunday program. These worksheets, some of which include prayers and readings, allow youth to express themselves through writing and roleplaying. Permission is granted to make copies of these pages for any person studying MISSION: CHRISTMAS.

Bible Studies. At the end of each Sunday program is a Bible study that will give your youth an in-depth look at the week's Scripture lesson. These studies are great for Sunday school lessons or midweek Bible studies and can help engage older youth. Each Bible study encourages teens to make connections between the week's Scripture and their daily lives. The Bible Dictionary on pages 78–80 will aid the groups using these studies, though having additional biblical reference materials on hand is recommended.

Advent Drama

Drama has a tendency to invoke emotion in ways that traditional worship experiences cannot. Therefore, MISSION: CHRISTMAS includes one easy-to-perform play for the Advent season. This drama, by Steve Butler, was originally written for and performed by the youth at Annandale United Methodist Church in Johnson City, Tennessee. Have your teens read through the play during a youth group meeting, or prepare a performance for your congregation. Permission is granted to make copies of these pages for any person studying MISSION: CHRISTMAS.

Worship Ideas

Worship, an important part of any season, fosters communal unity and individual nourishment of the spirit. MISSION: CHRISTMAS provides you with a variety of worship ideas that are perfect for Advent. From a simple lighting of Advent candles to a progressive nativity, these ideas will help you create Advent worship experiences that engage teens' senses and build community.

Service Projects

We often hear that "Christmas is a season of giving." And Christians have plenty of opportunities to contribute money, collect food and clothing, and volunteer their time during the holiday season. MISSION: CHRISTMAS gives you some creative service ideas that you can implement with your youth.

Party Plans

What would Christmas be without a Christmas party? MISSION: CHRISTMAS offers you help in putting together your youth ministry's annual Christmas party in a way that incorporates both fun and faith.

The season's other big party occasion is the celebration of the New Year. Unfortunately, many people behave irresponsibly on New Year's Eve, making going out for the holiday dangerous. MISSION: CHRISTMAS gives you a plan for putting together a safe New Year's celebration for your youth.

Both party plans are flexible and provide a variety of ideas and activities that are relevant to the holidays. More importantly, the plans give you a way to celebrate while helping the youth make connections between these special occasions and their faith.

Bible Dictionary

The three-page Bible Dictionary might better be described as a Bible glossary, because chances are that no Bible dictionary sitting on your bookshelf or in your church library contains only three pages.

But the Bible Dictionary provides more than just definitions. Each entry gives the user pertinent historical, geographical, and theological information, as well as relevant Scripture references.

The Bible Dictionary is designed to be used with the Bible studies at the end of each Sunday program, though you can use it to enhance several activities in this book. Permission is granted to make copies of the Bible Dictionary for any person studying MISSION: CHRISTMAS.

Advent Advice

Merry Cold, Dark Christmas

By Josh Tinley

To many Americans, a day in late fall or winter begins with the scraping of frost or ice from the car windshield. After a long day at school or work, many of us drive, ride, or walk home in darkness because the sun has set earlier that afternoon. So, why do we celebrate Advent—the season of preparation for the joyous gift of Christ—during this coldest and darkest time of year? Do we know that Jesus was born on December 25? For that matter, why do we begin each new year on January 1? Wouldn't we enjoy the holiday season more if it were in May?

Scripture says nothing about the time of year when Jesus was born, but the church has always recognized the Messiah's birth in the darkest days of winter. The original date of Christmas was January 6. It was changed to December 25 in the fourth century.

We know a little more about New Year's Day, which has been celebrated for millennia. The ancient Babylonians, who recognized the holiday as early as 2000 B.C., celebrated the beginning of each new year on the first day of spring. In Roman times, emperors had the power to change the calendar and begin a new year whenever they felt like doing so. The Roman Senate in 153 B.C. decided that the new year would begin on January 1. Julius Caesar affirmed this change when he introduced his Julian Calendar in 46 B.C. Unlike the Babylonian new year, the Roman new year had no seasonal or astronomical meaning.

Some ancient cultures, such as the Persians, chose to celebrate the birth of the sun at this time of year. The idea was that, on the shortest day of the year, the sun was in its infancy. From that point on, the sun would grow, lighting the sky for longer and longer periods each day until at last it began to fade. Through the late summer and fall, hours of sunlight would be replaced by hours of darkness. Then, toward the end of December, the sun would be born again.

It is interesting, then, that we celebrate Christmas during a season when some ancient peoples celebrated the birth of the light. Jesus is the "light of the world" (**John 8:12**), and when he came to earth, he illuminated a world overwhelmed by darkness. And in times of fear and sadness, when the light seems to be fading away, Christ can cut through the darkness and bring new light. It is also interesting that we begin each new year during this season. Even amid icy mornings and sunless afternoons, we can pause to reflect on the past year and look forward to the promises and opportunities of the year to come.

For much of the Advent season, the days will continually get shorter. Many youth will spend the weeks leading up to Christmas completing end-of-the-semester projects and papers and studying for final exams (though some have the misfortune of taking finals after Christmas). Teens who participate in winter sports will spend their afternoons in grueling practices or hard-fought competitions; youth who are involved in music and drama will likely be preparing school Christmas programs.

But students will be rewarded for their strife. That blessed time known at most schools as winter break is coming. During this two-week (give or take) vacation, teens will enjoy some much-needed rest, get some new stuff, and look forward to the promise of a new year. More importantly, they will be reminded of the ever-present hope that is theirs because God came to us so many years ago in the form of an infant child born in a stable.

The connection between the secular celebration of the new year, religiously-neutral winter breaks, and the sacred holiday of Christmas is not just a coincidence. Just as winter break provides relief from the burdens of schoolwork and after-school activities, Christ's birth offers relief from the burdens of sin and fear. And as New Year's Day signifies the promise and opportunity of a new year, Christmas signifies the promise and opportunity of a new age that began with the coming of the Messiah.

Advent is the time when we prepare to celebrate the coming of Christ—both in the form of an infant two thousand years ago and in all of the ways Christ continues to work within our lives and our world. Preparing for Christ's coming means telling the ancient stories of Mary and Joseph, the shepherds, and John the Baptist. We must also help our youth understand this season of cold, commercialism, and craziness in the context of the story of God's salvation. One way to do so is to take a closer look at how the church marks each Sunday during Advent.

First Sunday
The first Sunday in Advent looks forward to Christ's coming in final victory. This Sunday is the first of the Christian year, and it celebrates the beginning of our story by looking forward to the story's glorious conclusion.

Second Sunday
The second Sunday in Advent is usually devoted to the ministry of John the Baptist. We remember John as the one who "prepared the way of the Lord." John's ministry gave first-century Jews a glimpse of the one who would follow him. His story reminds us in the twenty-first century to prepare our hearts for Christ and to give others a glimpse of the one whom we follow.

Third Sunday
On the third Sunday in Advent, we celebrate how God's promises—to the patriarchs, the Old Testament prophets, Elizabeth and Zechariah, Mary and Joseph, and us today—are fulfilled in the gift of Jesus Christ. In our darkest days (literally and figuratively), we have hope because of Jesus' life, death, and resurrection.

Fourth Sunday
The fourth Sunday of Advent is a day for us to tell the story of Jesus' birth. On this Sunday, we recall the journey to Bethlehem, the inn that was filled to capacity, the angels who proclaimed Jesus' coming, and the shepherds in the fields who rushed to visit the blessed child. Of course, Christ's coming was not just a one-time event. Christ is born over and again in the hearts of his followers.

Christmas Sunday
The Sunday after Christmas is a day of praise and thanksgiving for God's greatest gift. Our season of preparation culminates in a celebration of God coming to us as the infant child born in a Bethlehem stable.

While youth are slipping on ice or watching four o'clock sunsets, they can be assured that, soon, the days will grow longer and the weather warmer. As they cram for exams and scramble to finish end-of-the-semester assignments, they can look forward to a new semester and a fresh start. Those of us who work with youth need to make them aware of a greater truth: Because of God's gift of Jesus Christ, they have been given a fresh start, and they can always look forward to brighter days.

First Sunday

The First Sunday of Advent

Key Verse: "Therefore you also must be ready, for the Son of Man is coming at an unexpected hour" (**Matthew 24:44**).

Old Testament: Isaiah 2:1-4 (Return to God, who is gracious and merciful.)

New Testament: Matthew 24:36-44 ("Keep awake therefore, for you do not know on what day your Lord is coming.")

Christ Is Coming!

Advent is all about getting ready. To think of Advent simply as the opening act for the Christmas season is to miss the point. Advent is not part of Christmas; Advent prepares us for Christmas.

Unfortunately, even in the church, many youth (and adults) think little of the Advent season. If they think of it at all, it probably brings to mind only Christmas parties, nativity scenes, and maybe a Chrismon tree or extra church services. And while teens might associate Advent with the coming of Christ, they likely think of Jesus' coming only as a baby in the manger. But in reality the nativity is not even half of the story. Advent is about preparing for the coming of Christ in glorious ways—not just Jesus "the infant meek and mild" but also Christ the ruler and judge of creation.

Of course, popular media can distort a youth's perspective of Advent. In the weeks (and months) before Christmas, advertising campaigns sketch a materialistic picture of how we should prepare for Christmas. Many retailers enjoy big profits during the Advent season. Marketing has become such a major part of the season that people often forget that Advent is not just a few weeks in which to finish shopping for Christmas presents, to wrap boxes, or to mail cards. We must remind youth and others in our congregations that Advent is a grace period God offers to faithful disciples of Christ during which we are to prepare our hearts and minds for the coming of the one who makes more difference than any video game, MP3 player, or new outfit ever could.

The color purple, which many churches display during Advent, conveys passion and deep emotion, representing bruised souls and broken spirits. But since purple is also a color of royalty and power, it links the pain and suffering of the world (including the struggles of youth) to the Lord and King, who promises to bring grace, justice, and healing.

How are you preparing for Christ's coming?

Advent also offers us a chance to examine how we use our time. Youth who spend much of Advent burdened with school and extracurricular activities may feel as though their schedules leave no room for flexibility. But this season of preparation should not be taken for granted even in the midst of final exams, basketball games, and school music programs. Teens (and the adults who work with them) should be encouraged to set aside time—whether early in the morning, late at night, during study breaks, or after practice—to spend with God, serve others, and prepare their hearts for Christ's coming.

Devotion to God is important year-round. But since Advent begins the Christian calendar, it is a good time to evaluate how we are doing, to determine what changes we need to make, and to prepare ourselves for the one who comes as Lord of all nations and peoples.

First Sunday

Mission Plan

Activity	Supplies
<u>Light the First Advent Candle</u>	• Advent wreath with candles • Bible • matches
<u>Prepare!</u>	• blank sheets of paper • notecards • chalkboard, markerboard, or large sheet of paper • pens or pencils • marker or piece of chalk
<u>Signs of the (Advent) Season</u>	• copies of Signs of the (Advent) Season handout (page 46) • pens or pencils • large writing surface • marker or piece of chalk
<u>Get Ready for Whom?</u>	• Bibles • blank sheets of paper • pencils • colored pencils or markers • large writing surface • marker or piece of chalk
<u>God of All the Nations</u>	• Bibles
<u>Stay Focused!</u>	• large writing surface (optional) • marker or chalk (optional)
<u>Closing Prayer</u>	• paper • scissors • pens or pencils • hat or container

---

<u>Bible Study: Matthew 24:36-44</u>

You will need Bibles, paper, scissors, and pens or pencils. Optional: a large writing surface and chalk or a marker.

You Will Need

- Advent wreath and candles that you will be able to use throughout the season. (For more information on Advent wreaths, see page 78.)
- Bible
- match

*Adapted from *From Hope to Joy.* Copyright © 1984 by Abingdon Press. Used by permission.

You Will Need

- sheets of paper
- chalkboard, markerboard, or sheet of paper
- pens or pencils
- marker or piece of chalk

Beforehand, write on separate sheets of paper some or all of the preparation-requiring events below. (You may wish to provide additional or different situations your group considers important.)

- high school graduation
- a wedding
- the birth of a child
- starting a new job
- taking a long vacation
- taking an exam

You Will Need

- copies of Signs of the (Advent) Season handout (page 46)
- pens or pencils
- large writing surface
- marker or piece of chalk

Light the First Advent Candle

Begin this session by using the following short service:

1. Have a volunteer read aloud **Isaiah 60:1-3.**

2. Light the first Advent candle.

3. Ask another volunteer to read:

> We light this candle as a symbol of Christ our Hope.
> May the light sent from God shine in the darkness
> to show us the way of salvation.
> O come, O come, Emmanuel.*

Prepare!

In their lifetime, people prepare for many events, milestones, and occasions. Understanding the importance of getting ready for some of these events will help youth better understand the importance of preparing to celebrate God's gift of Jesus Christ during Advent.

Divide the teens into groups of three or four, and give each group one of the sheets (see the margin) and a pen or pencil. Instruct the youth to list on a sheet of paper what someone would need to do to prepare adequately for the task on their card.

Allow the youth several minutes to make their lists; then invite each group to read its responses. If you have more than one group, ask a member of each group to record its list on a markerboard, chalkboard, or large sheet of paper. After each presentation, invite members of any other groups to add items to the list.

Once every group has presented its list, remind the youth that the Advent season is the church's time to prepare for the arrival of Jesus Christ into the world and into our hearts. Also remind them that just as events in our lives require preparation, we can do many things to get ourselves ready to live and grow as faithful disciples of Christ.

Signs of the (Advent) Season

Distribute copies of the Signs of the (Advent) Season handout (page 46) and pens or pencils. Invite the youth to individually spend a few minutes brainstorming items to list in each quadrant of the circle on the handout. Completing this exercise will help the youth see similarities and differences among the ways various sectors of society mark the approach of Christmas.

When most of the teens have finished, come together as a group and create a composite four-quadrant circle on a large writing surface.

Take time to compare the lists in the quadrants. Discuss the significance of each item on each list and what each one means to its respective sector of society. For instance:

✝ The symbolic decorations put up during a Hanging of the Greens service emphasizes to the church that Christ is the focal point of Christmas.

✝ A family might use an Advent wreath at home to mark progress toward Christ's arrival as the light of the world.

✝ The shopping mall might use Santa Claus, elf characters, and other secular decorations to attract shoppers and rack up big sales.

✝ The media would likely mark the season by airing holiday specials and Christmas-movie favorites to get viewers into the holiday spirit.

When you are finished, ask:

✝ Which of the types of preparation we have listed most exemplify the true meaning of Christmas?

✝ Which of these items might distract us from the true meaning of Christmas?

Get Ready for Whom?

Divide the youth into small groups. (You might have them get into their groups from Prepare!) Give each group at least one Bible; then say: "Advent is a season of preparation, so we need to think about what we're preparing for. Since we're getting ready for the coming of Jesus Christ, we need to think about who Christ was and is."

Instruct the groups to work together to create a picture of Jesus Christ. They may come up with a written description, or they may literally draw a picture. The groups may also present Christ in another manner, such as through a skit or a song. Encourage creativity, but also encourage the youth to use their Bibles and to incorporate Scripture into their creations.

Have each group present its picture of Christ. Then have all of the youth list on a large writing surface the various names and titles for Jesus Christ (such as Emmanuel, the Prince of Peace, and the Son of God) and the roles Christ plays (such as healer, teacher, and Savior).

Say: "Christ is called by many names and titles and has played many roles. He continues to relate to people in various ways." Ask the youth to silently reflect on these questions for a few minutes:

✝ How does Jesus Christ speak to you?

✝ What roles does Jesus Christ play in your life?

You Will Need
- Bibles
- blank sheets of paper
- pencils
- colored pencils or markers
- large writing surface
- marker or piece of chalk

Suggestion: For ways to help the youth deepen their understanding of the temptations Jesus faced, see the Bible study (page 14).

You Will Need
- large writing surface (optional)
- marker or piece of chalk (optional)

God of All the Nations

Distribute the Bibles, and have the youth read (silently or aloud) **Isaiah 2:1-4.** Say: "The God we meet in Christ—the God we worship—is a big God whose work began long before Jesus came to earth. God is not only the God of Jesus' followers but also of the Hebrews from whom we have received our Old Testament. But God is far more than just the God of the Hebrews and early Christians. God is the creator of the world and the Lord of the universe. Our God lays claim to everyone and everything." Ask:

✝ According to Isaiah's vision, what kind of future did God have planned for the world and its peoples?

✝ How was God working in the world to make Isaiah's vision a reality?

Say: "The God whom Isaiah knew, served, and spoke for is the same God who came to the world in Jesus Christ. When we prepare for Jesus' birth, we are not only getting ready to welcome a baby in a manger. Rather, we are preparing to welcome the ruler of creation who comes to bring peace on earth and in our hearts."

Stay Focused!

Say: "Advent gives Christians an entire season to focus on the power, mystery, and meaning of God's incarnation in Jesus Christ. Yet we can easily become distracted while preparing to welcome God's holy child." Ask, "What can distract Christians from focusing on Christ during Advent?" (Answers may include final exams, family tensions Christmas shopping, and over-the-top decorations.) You might list on a large writing surface the teens' answers to the question above.

Say, "So that we can give our full attention this Advent to God's incarnation in Jesus Christ, we are going to practice staying focused."

Select one youth, and give this person a simple task to perform such as saying the Lord's Prayer or singing a common Christmas hymn. Instruct the rest of the group to be silent, and invite the "focus youth" to perform this task.

After the task is complete, ask for several volunteers to be distracters. Their job will be to break the focus youth's concentration so that he or she cannot complete the assigned task. Allow the distracters to sing loudly, dance, tell jokes, or choose other disruptive activities, but clearly tell the distracters they should not touch the focus youth.

Invite the focus youth to perform his or her task again, this time with the distracters trying to break his or her concentration.

Repeat this exercise several times, choosing different focus youth and distracters. You might try variations on this game such as having two or more focus youth work together to perform a given task.

When you are finished, ask the teens who were focus youth:

✝ Whom or what did you find most distracting?

✝ What was the most effective way you found to block out the distractions?

Then ask everyone, "What can we as Christians do to eliminate distractions during Advent?" (Answers may include prayer, worship, acts of service, and putting up decorations that celebrate the spiritual side of the holidays.)

Closing Prayer

Give each youth a slip of paper, and instruct the teens to write their name on their slip. Collect all of the slips, put them in a hat or other container, and have each youth draw one slip. (If a youth draws his or her own name, have him or her draw again.)

Say: "One way to stay focused during Advent is to make prayer a daily habit. I would like each of you to make an effort to pray every day and to commit to including in your daily prayers the person whose slip of paper you drew."

Close by having a volunteer read aloud the following prayer:

O God of All the Nations,

You have come to this world in Jesus Christ, our Lord. In this season of Advent, prepare our hearts, minds, bodies, and souls, to love and serve you in all we do. Help us to focus on your love and grace, so that we may share it with everyone we meet. Amen.

You Will Need
- paper
- scissors
- pens or pencils
- hat or other container

Beforehand, cut the paper into slips.

Bible Study

Matthew 24:36-44

You will need *Bibles, paper, scissors, and pencils or pens. Optional: a large writing surface and chalk or a marker. Beforehand, cut the paper into small slips.*

On a large writing surface, write *EXPECT THE UNEXPECTED* in large letters. Ask the youth to brainstorm examples of things that happen unexpectedly. As the group calls out ideas, write them below the heading you have written. The ideas may range from joyous (such as a surprise party) to tragic (such as a sudden illness or injury). You might record these examples in separate columns, according to what kind of unexpected events are mentioned. Allow plenty of time for the students to generate responses.

Then say: "Advent is a time to prepare for the coming of Jesus Christ, not just as a baby in a manger. During Advent we need to think about what it means to prepare for Christ to come again as the Savior of the world who judges evil and establishes justice and peace. We are going to look at one Scripture the church uses to prepare for all of the ways Christ comes to us."

Distribute the Bibles. Divide the youth into groups of three or four. Have one member of each group read aloud **Matthew 24:36-44** while the others follow along. Have the groups read the Scripture a second time, this time with another member reading aloud.

Instruct the youth to discuss these questions, which you may write on a large writing surface:

✝ Have you ever had someone try to convince you he or she knew when Jesus would return? How did you respond?

✝ According to Scripture, who truly knows when Jesus will come again? (only God the Father)

✝ Besides returning to earth as a human being, in what other ways does Christ come to people?

✝ How good of a job do you usually do of preparing yourself to receive Christ? How could you better prepare yourself to welcome Christ in whatever way he comes to you?

Invite one person from each group to summarize for everyone his or her group's discussion.

Next, reread aloud **Matthew 24:37-39** for all of the youth. Then say: "Jesus drew a comparison between his coming and the unexpected way the Great Flood came upon people in the story of Noah from **Genesis 6–7.** The people in Noah's day were doing ordinary things such as eating, drinking, and getting married, with no clue that God's judgment was coming. Christ warns us to always live in a such a way that we would be glad for him to come to us."

Have the group rewrite **Matthew 24:38-39,** replacing "eating and drinking, marrying and giving in marriage" with daily mundane activities the teens do. The resulting passage might look like this: "For, as in those days before the flood, they were going to school and soccer practice, playing video games, and talking on the telephone, until the day Noah entered the ark, and they knew nothing until the flood came and swept them all away, so too will be the coming of the Son of Man."

Finally, distribute small slips of paper to the group. Instruct the youth to write on the slips one thing they can do during Advent to be better prepared to welcome Jesus. Examples could include, "read my Bible daily," "pray each morning," and "worship each week." Ask the youth to commit to doing each day during Advent what they have written and to keep their slip of paper where they will see it.

Close the Bible study with a prayer asking God to help you and your youth always be prepared for Christ's coming.

14

Second Sunday

The Second Sunday of Advent

Key Verse: "In those days John the Baptist appeared in the wilderness of Judea, proclaiming, 'Repent, for the kingdom of heaven has come near.' " (**Matthew 3:1-2**).

Old Testament: **Isaiah 40:1-11**
(God's people are comforted by God's promises.)

New Testament: **Matthew 3:1-12**
(John the Baptist prepares the way of Christ.)

Prepare the Way of the Lord

If you have ever gone to a concert—whether rock, country, hip-hop, or gospel—you have probably seen an opening act take the stage before the main attraction. Openers warm up the audience and get them excited about the star who will follow. These acts must humbly accept being less popular performers than the featured acts. Opening a concert lacks the glory and prestige of headlining but is important nonetheless.

The gospel has an opening act too. John the Baptist hits the stage before Jesus, the headliner, bursts onto the scene. All four Gospels mention John's ministry at the beginning of Jesus' story and agree that John prepared "the way of the Lord"; Luke even tells the story of John's birth.

Scholars can only guess what religious groups John may have belonged to or where he might have lived. But the Gospel record and other historical sources suggest that John clearly had built a large following (whether or not he had intended to). All types of people came out to the wilderness to hear John and to be baptized.

Established religious leaders and teachers of the day showed up to see this charismatic and enigmatic prophet. Some scholars think that even Jesus followed John before taking center stage himself. Who knows what John could have done as a solo act?

John may well have struggled with a temptation many of us struggle with: to live and seek glory for ourselves and our accomplishments. But the primary purpose of John's ministry was not glory or fame. Instead, he proclaimed the same deceptively simple message with which Jesus began his public ministry: "Repent, for the kingdom of heaven has come near" (**Matthew 3:2, Matthew 4:17b**). John devoted his mission entirely to God and God's hopes for the world. He called all people to turn from whatever distracted them from God.

John knew that the real star of the show was yet to come. His job was to prepare people for the pinnacle of God's action in the world. Though John died prematurely at the hands of King Herod, his work did not end in the first century; it continues now. Every Advent season, we hear John's voice echoing, "Repent" from the wilderness just beyond the boundaries of our everyday lives. He calls us back to prepare for the one who comes into the world and into our lives to make God's kingdom a reality. Listen closely, and you will hear John. Heed his call, take up his work, and prepare the way of the Lord!

> **How can you "prepare the way of the Lord"?**

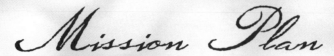

Mission Plan

Activity	Supplies
Light the Second Advent Candle	• Advent wreath • Bible • matches
Who Gets You Ready?	• paper • pens or pencils
Worship Prepares Us	• enough church bulletins from a recent worship service for every youth to have one
Good News and Bad News	No supplies needed
A Voice Cries Out for God	• Bibles
Remember Your Baptism	• bowl or other container that can hold water • small seashells or small, smooth stones • hymnal (optional)
Closing Prayer	No supplies needed

Bible Study: Matthew 3:1-12

You will need Bibles, paper, and pens or pencils.

Light the Second Advent Candle

Begin this session by using the following short service:

1. Have a volunteer read aloud **Mark 1:4.**

2. Light the first and second Advent candles.

3. Ask another volunteer to read aloud:

> We light this candle as a symbol of Christ the Way.
> May the Word sent from God through the prophets
>   lead us to the way of salvation.
> O come, O come, Emmanuel.*

Who Gets You Ready?

Use the following information to introduce the youth to the story of John the Baptist:

> John the Baptist came to get people ready for Jesus' ministry. Though John played a unique role in the story of our faith, the Bible tells stories of many people God sent as prophets and messengers. The work of these servants of God was often difficult but always straightforward: telling folks that God wanted their attention. Many of us know the difficulty of finding our way back to God when we get off on the wrong track. We need others to prepare us for God's presence in our lives.

Say: "From an early age, we are surrounded by people of influence preparing us for life's challenges. When you were young children, your family gradually prepared you to move beyond the household and cope with the world. Now teachers help you develop the knowledge and skills you need to contribute to society. Coaches help you hone your physical abilities. Scout leaders may provide you with training in leadership and responsibility. Pastors and youth ministers help you prepare for a lifetime of spiritual growth and development that will enable you to become devoted disciples of Jesus Christ and faithful servants of God and neighbor."

Distribute sheets of paper and pens or pencils. Ask the students to think about people who have influenced their lives—especially those people who have helped them prepare for something important that they have done or hope to do in the future.

Instruct the youth to choose one such person and to write a paragraph about the most helpful thing that person has shown or taught them. Encourage them to write about how what they have learned from that person will affect their life in the future. Give the youth plenty of time to work; then allow volunteers to read aloud their paragraphs.

Notes

You Will Need
- Advent wreath
- Bible
- matches

*Adapted from *From Hope to Joy*. Copyright © 1984 by Abingdon Press. Used by permission.

You Will Need
- paper
- pens or pencils

Notes

You Will Need

- enough church bulletins from a recent worship service for every youth to have one

If you can do so beforehand, invite to the session someone from your congregation who regularly plans worship, such as a pastor, music minister, or member of the worship committee.

Worship Prepares Us

Say: "In a sense, a worship service is an ongoing preparation for what comes next. For example, many services begin with a musical prelude that allows us to prepare quietly and prayerfully to offer ourselves to God. A spoken call to worship or responsive reading may invite us to gather for a sacred time. An opening hymn may set the tone for the service by inviting us to sing about a particular theme of the service. Prayers are offered to prepare us to hear Scriptures, listen to sermons, give offerings, or commit to discipleship. At the end of the service, a special hymn or benediction reminds us of the theme of the service and prepares us to return to the world to serve God and others."

Divide the youth into groups of three or four. Have each group examine different parts of the worship service outlined on a recent worship bulletin by asking, "What does this segment prepare us for?" While there are no right answers to this question, go from group to group to make sure that the youth understand that the different components of your church's worship have a purpose. If your pastor or other worship planner is available to help the youth to understand the movements and goals of a worship service, ask him or her to go from group to group, offering ideas and answering questions.

Option: Have the youth plan a service of worship that would be appropriate for the Advent season. Use the Prepare to Worship handouts (pages 48–49) as a template for the service; the youth may add to the template or make their own, as long as your pastor or priest approves of these contributions. If a guest "worship expert" has joined you for Worship Prepares Us, ask that person to assist the youth in choosing hymns, prayers, and Scriptures, with an eye toward helping the worshipers prepare to receive the gift of Christ.

Good News and Bad News

Say: "John the Baptist proclaimed that the kingdom of heaven was near. But he also called people to repent of anything that stood between them and the lives God had called them to lead. One could say that John brought good news and bad news: the good news of God's kingdom and the bad news that all was not right with the world and people's lives. But even John's bad news came with a kernel of good news: People are sinful, but God is willing to forgive."

Have the youth pair off, and instruct the pairs to create a brief skit in which they deliver a message similar to John's message. Challenge them think of a situation in which they are delivering news that could be seen as bad news on the surface but contains a measure of good news. For example, a father could tell his daughter that she is being grounded for getting a D in algebra but that he is also going to set aside time to help her every day so that she can raise her grade.

The students may think of serious or light-hearted examples. Give the pairs about five minutes to prepare; then ask each pair to present its skit. After each skit ask the youth to name the good news and the bad news that was presented.

A Voice Cries Out for God

Hand out Bibles, and ask volunteers to read aloud **Isaiah 40:1-11** one or two verses at a time. Then ask:

✟ Whose voice do you imagine "crying out" (verses 3 and 6)?

✟ How would you describe God's attitude in this Scripture toward God's people?

✟ Isaiah was addressing a certain group of people. How would you describe their attitude toward God?

✟ What are the similarities between the message proclaimed in **Isaiah 40:1-11** and John's message in **Matthew 3:1-12**?

✟ What are some ways God calls God's people to repent and receive forgiveness today?

Say: "Isaiah probably wrote this Scripture in the middle of the sixth century B.C. John proclaimed his message almost six hundred years later. Still today, we are called to 'prepare the way of the Lord' by repenting of our sins and doing the work of God's kingdom on earth."

Remember Your Baptism

If you have invited a member of the clergy to be part of other portions of this session, it would be appropriate (and in some traditions, necessary) to ask her or him to remain and preside over this activity.

Say: "Many Christian rites and ceremonies are geared toward making us ready to take another step in faith. What rituals and practices prepare us for the various steps along our Christian journeys?" (Answers may include Communion, Sunday school, confirmation, and small groups.)

Say: "While various denominations and individual Christians sometimes disagree on what practices are important and meaningful, most Christians believe baptism is one of our most sacred rituals. It is the sacrament by which persons are publicly claimed by God and initiated into the body of Christ. Baptism is one of the first steps in preparing for a lifetime of Christian devotion, service, and growth. And while the baptism John the Baptist administered was not identical to the Christian baptism we know today, the church's baptismal practices are rooted in John's work as he prepared the way for Jesus."

You Will Need
• Bibles

You Will Need
• bowl or other container that can hold water
• small seashells or small, smooth stones
• hymnal (optional)

Beforehand, fill the container will small stones or seashells and water.

Note: This activity is not an appropriate time to conduct actual baptisms unless significant planning and communication among youth, parents, and pastoral authorities have been done ahead of time.

Consult your congregation or denomination's hymnal or book of worship for a service for the reaffirmation of baptismal vows. You may also use the model below. If your tradition requires an ordained clergyperson to preside at such a service, make appropriate arrangements beforehand.

Keep in mind that most likely, not all of your youth will have had identical baptismal experiences. Some may have been baptized as infants, others only recently, and still others not at all. Nevertheless, all of the youth should be invited to participate in some way and should be allowed to abstain if they wish. This service is intended only as remembrance of baptism, not as a baptism or re-baptism. Yet the grace of God that is present in the sacrament of baptism is also experienced in services of baptismal remembrance.

A Short Service of Baptismal Remembrance

Leader: *Through the sacrament of baptism, we are made part of Christ's holy church and included in the family of God. We are the recipients of God's grace even before we know it, and we rejoice to be part of the body of Christ.*

Read **Matthew 3:13-17.**

Leader: *In baptism, Jesus was proclaimed as God's beloved child and was assured that he found favor with the Almighty. After the example of Christ, we too were claimed by God in our baptism.*

The waters of baptism are a powerful symbol. They remind us of the waters of chaos that covered the earth as God began to create the world, of the destructive waters that flooded the earth when Noah and his family were spared, of the sea that was parted so that the children of Israel might escape to freedom, and of the water of the mother's womb in which Jesus our Lord was nurtured. We thank God for the gift of this water and the new life in Jesus Christ that it symbolizes. As we pause now to reflect on the gift of love that God has granted, remember your baptism and be thankful.

At this point, the participants may come to the water and touch it, take a seashell or stone from the container, or touch the water and make the mark of the cross on their forehead.

Leader: *Let us pray together: "God, we thank you for all that you have given us. We thank you for our baptism and our place in your church. Hold us close, and prepare us for the life you call us to live in Christ's name. Amen."*

Closing Prayer

Close your time together by having a volunteer pray this prayer:

Gracious Lord,

As John the Baptist called people to repent long ago, you continue to call us to turn to you in love and service. Give us the courage, strength, patience, and grace to give ourselves to you as you have given yourself to us. In Christ's name, amen.

Bible Study

Matthew 3:1-12

You will need *Bibles, paper, and pens or pencils.*

Say: "Sometimes, understanding the opposite of what a Scripture says helps us better understand what the passage is saying and why it is important."

Divide the youth into a number of teams that is a multiple of three (three, six, nine, and so on). Make sure that no more than four persons are on any team. To one third of the teams, assign **Matthew 3:1-6;** to another third, assign **Matthew 3:7-10;** and to the final third, assign **Matthew 3:11-12.** (If you have fewer than five youth, assign each individual youth a Scripture.)

Hand out paper and writing utensils. Instruct the teams to read and re-read their verses until they have a clear sense of what is being said. Then have the teams write a negative version of their assigned Scriptures. For example, a negative rewrite of **Matthew 3:11-12** might say: "I do not baptize you for repentance, because nobody with any power is coming after me. The one who follows me is nothing special. He does not care what people do or how they live. And he certainly won't punish those who are unfaithful."

Give the teams plenty of time to work. When they have finished, group the teams or individuals into larger groups so that each large group includes one team or person from each third. (If you have fewer than five youth, have everyone work as one team.) Instruct the large groups to string together their three negative Scriptures so that they have a complete negative rewrite of **Matthew 3:1-12.** Allow the large groups a few minutes to tweak their rewritten Scriptures; then instruct them to write their entire negative version of the Scripture on a large writing surface. Invite a volunteer from each large group to read aloud his or her group's rewrite.

Then discuss the Scripture using the following questions:

✝ Why does John the Baptist call us to repent?

✝ What does repenting of something involve?

✝ Can you think of examples of persons whose lives changed significantly when they repented? Explain.

✝ John the Baptist's appearance sounds like it was out of the ordinary. Who in our world today might seem as weird as John the Baptist? How might you respond to this person if he or she told you to repent and prepare for the coming of the Lord?

✝ Who are the "John the Baptists" in your life? Who holds you accountable for how you live as a Christian?

✝ People confessed their sins when they went to be baptized by John. What is the value in confessing our sins to God?

✝ John the Baptist warned people that they should not count on their heritage to win God's favor (**Matthew 3:9**). What about your life causes you to think "I'm OK. I don't need to change"? How do these things distract you from hearing God's voice?

✝ The Bible and the church teach that Christ gives us grace and forgiveness but also, as John the Baptist suggested, brings judgment (**Matthew 3:12**). How might Christ judge you? our culture? What might he tell us we need to change?

Say: "No matter how well things are going or how good we feel we are, we always need to listen to voices like John's, which calls us to repent and draw closer to God. The Christian life is one of constant preparation for God's coming kingdom, and we always have room to grow spiritually."

Close by praying and checking in with how the youth are keeping up with the prayers they began last week for a group member.

Third Sunday

The Third Sunday of Advent

Key Verse: "For nothing will be impossible with God" (**Luke 1:37**).

Old Testament: Zephaniah 3:14-20 (A song of joy for Israel)

New Testament: Luke 1:26-38 (Gabriel foretells Jesus' birth.)

Things As They Truly Are

First impressions can be deceiving. Something helpful may look dangerous, and something harmful may look pleasant and enticing.

For example, say you are walking in the woods one afternoon, looking for flowers and greenery to take home as a decorative bouquet. You find lots of pretty flowers for your collection. Then you come upon an attractive vine with green leaves and lovely white berries. You pick some of this foliage for the bouquet and head home. A few minutes later, you start itching. Red spots appear on your arm, and soon you are in agony. The attractive, green vine with the white berries is in fact poison ivy; your first impression had been wrong.

On the other hand, take the three-toed sloth, a South American mammal. The first thing most people would notice about this beast are the long, sharp claws at the end of its lengthy arms. If you were unfamiliar with the sloth, you might think it was a vicious, aggressive animal with bladelike weapons for fingers. But a sloth is an extraordinarily slow animal; it lives in trees and uses its long claws to hang upside down and eat

leaves. Even if it were vicious, a sloth would be too slow to attack. Though it looks ferocious, the animal is docile. It is not what it seems.

In Luke's Gospel, Mary the mother of Jesus had her own experience with first impressions that don't tell the entire story. You know Mary's story: The angel Gabriel came to Mary, told her not to be afraid, and informed her that she would give birth to the Messiah—God's own Son—even though she was a virgin.

At first, Gabriel's news was more distressing than promising to this young girl. Since women at this time were betrothed and married at a young age, Mary was likely no older than age thirteen. She was a kid, or a junior high youth, if you will.

Where do you find God in times of uncertainty?

Imagine if a seventh- or eighth-grade girl in your church were told that she was pregnant even though she had never had a boyfriend, much less intercourse, and that God had chosen her to bear and raise the promised Christ child. Many mature adults would find such responsibility terrifying, or at least intimidating. Mary has to cope with it as a young girl. Although a woman Mary's age giving birth would not have been shocking in her day, the role of mother of God was still a lot for a young girl to deal with.

In spite of this difficulty, Mary's had her Jewish heritage. She had heard her people tell stories of how God had over and over again miraculously transformed seemingly hopeless situations into signs of God's love and promises. Scripture is full of such stories. Mary's predicament is just another one of those misleading occasions when God's plans for good are difficult to recognize at first.

Seeing the good and the promise in a situation that otherwise appears hopeless takes faith, courage, and an understanding of the stories of God's people. Mary could have allowed fear to consume her, but she knew that her God was the God who had repeatedly rescued God's people, bringing victory out of almost certain defeat, joy out of sorrow, and hope out of despair. Her God was the God about whom the prophet Zephaniah had written,

> The Lord, your God, is in your midst,
> a warrior who gives victory;
> [the Lord] will rejoice over you with gladness,
> [God] will renew you in his love.
>   (**Zephaniah 3:17**)

Mary's story deals not only with a miraculous birth; it also deals with astounding faith, profound vision, and trust in God's will. Mary could have simply told Gabriel no. Instead she said, "Here am I, the servant of the Lord; let it be with me according to your word" (**Luke 1:38a**). She saw things as they truly were with God: full of hope, promise, life, and goodness.

In this lesson, help your youth see how God's greatest act began with someone they can relate to: a youth dealing with overwhelming pressure. Mary, like John the Baptist, was another servant of God who helps us prepare the way of the Lord!

Mission Plan

Activity	Supplies
Light the Third Advent Candle	• Advent wreath • Bible • matches
A Fantastic Story	• paper • pens or pencils • markers or colored pencils • Bible
Nothing Will Be Impossible With God	• copies of Impossible . . . or Maybe Not handout (page 47) • pens or pencils • large writing surface • paper
The Most Amazing Thing	• Bibles
Words of Hope and Promise	• Bibles • either paper and pens or pencils, or a large writing surface and markers or chalk
Learning to Trust	• slips of paper (optional) • pens or pencils (optional)
Closing Prayer	No supplies needed

Bible Study: Luke 1:5-9

You will need paper, a pen or pencil, a large writing surface, chalk or dry-erase markers, and Bibles.

You Will Need
- Advent wreath
- Bible
- matches

*From *From Hope to Joy.* Copyright ©
1984 by Abingdon Press. Used by
permission.

You Will Need
- paper
- pens or pencils
- markers or colored pencils
- Bible

Light the Third Advent Candle

Begin this session by lighting the first three Advent candles and
using the following short service:

1. Have a volunteer read **Isaiah 35:10.**
2. Light the first, second, and third Advent candles.
3. Ask another volunteer to read aloud:

> We light this candle as a symbol of Christ our Joy.
> May the joyful promise of your presence, O God,
>   make us rejoice in our hope of salvation.
> O come, O come, Emmanuel.*

A Fantastic Story

Hand out paper, pens or pencils, and markers or colored pencils.
Tell the teens to work individually or in pairs to create a fantastic story
that would be difficult to believe. The students may tell their story
by writing, illustrating, or creating a brief skit with a partner.

Give the youth plenty of time to work; then allow volunteers to
read or present their work. After the youth have told their stories,
say: "Imagine for a moment that you do not know the story of
Jesus. Pretend that you know nothing of the church's beginnings,
the great apostles, or the spread of Christianity. Imagine that you
have never heard about Mary, Joseph, or the virgin birth." Allow
youth to pause for a moment to get into this mindset. Then have
one or more volunteers read aloud **Luke 1:26-38.** Ask:

- How does your impression of this story change when you
  pretend to know nothing about Jesus' story?

- In what ways is Mary's story a fantastic story?

- How, do you think, would you feel if you were in Mary's
  situation? What would you have trouble believing? What would
  you find frightening?

Say: "This story is fantastic, not in the sense of being wonderfully
good but in the sense that we wouldn't normally believe such a
story. It includes messages from a supernatural being and a virgin
conceiving a child; and it demonstrates that God would choose to
do God's most important act through an otherwise unimportant
young girl who was about to be married to an otherwise
unimportant man.

"Of course, you do know the whole story of Jesus' birth and how Mary's initial story fits into the larger narrative of Jesus' life and work. On top of that, the church has had two millennia during which to tell Mary's story. But pretending to hear it for the first time can give the story new power and meaning. God's work is stunning, shocking, and unexpected. God works in the world in amazing, unbelievable, and fantastic ways!"

Nothing Will Be Impossible With God

Say: "When Gabriel tells Mary that she will have a child, she doesn't believe him. 'What? That's impossible!' Mary replies. The angel's response boils down to one straightforward answer: 'For God, nothing is impossible.' In other words, when it comes to God expressing God's love for the world, do not count out anything!"

Divide the youth into groups of four or five, and distribute the writing utensils and copies of Impossible . . . or Maybe Not handout (page 47). (If you have seven or fewer youth, work as one group.) Instruct the groups to work together to complete the handout by thinking of things that were once thought to be impossible. For example, a few hundred years ago, getting light from a source other than the sun, moon, stars, or fire would have seemed impossible to many. A thousand years ago, printing several identical copies of books would have seemed unlikely to most people. Just ten years ago, the thought of having one handheld device that could make phone calls, send messages, play games and music, and take pictures may have seemed ridiculous.

Give the groups plenty of time to work; then allow them to present their responses. Compile a group list on a large writing surface.

Next, distribute paper and invite the groups to complete the following statement on a separate sheet of paper or simply aloud in their groups: "I once thought that _____ was impossible for even God to do in my life."

For some youth, completing this statement may remind them of an uplifting story they can tell the other members of their group. Others may still have things in their lives that they think are impossible for even God to bring about. Give the students plenty of time to discuss this statement in their groups. Conclude this exercise by affirming with your teens that nothing is impossible when it comes to God caring for and loving God's people.

Notes

You Will Need
- copies of Impossible . . . or Maybe Not handout (page 47)
- pens or pencils
- large writing surface
- paper

The Most Amazing Thing

Say, "The announcement of Jesus' impending birth is by no means the only amazing story in the Bible." Distribute the Bibles, and divide the youth into small groups. (You may allow them to stay in groups from the previous activity.) Instruct the groups to scan their Bibles for some examples of amazing stories. Have each group select one or two stories that it finds especially fantastic.

Old Testament examples might include the Creation stories or the Great Flood in Genesis, Moses leading the Israelites through the Red Sea in Exodus, the tales of Samson in Judges, the accounts of Elijah and Elisha in First and Second Kings, or the stories of Ruth and Esther. The New Testament includes several amazing stories about Jesus, and the Book of Acts recounts some incredible events in the lives of the first disciples. The Book of Revelation contains many fantastic stories. Give the teens several minutes to work; then have the groups summarize their amazing stories for the others.

Next, say: "Amazing stories aren't limited to the Bible. God continues to do many fantastic things today." Ask:

✝ What amazing works of God have you experienced in your life or seen in the lives of others?
✝ How can a knowledge of the stories in the Bible help us better see how God is doing amazing things in our lives?

Words of Hope and Promise

Hand out the Bibles, and ask a volunteer to read aloud **Zephaniah 3:14-20** while the other youth follow along.

Either in small groups or as a whole group, list any words or phrases from this Scripture that convey good news from God. (If you have small groups, hand out a piece of paper and a writing utensil to each group. If you are compiling this list with the whole group, use a large writing surface.) Examples include verse 14 ("Rejoice and exult with all your heart") and verse 16 ("Do not fear").

Then discuss the following questions:

✝ What do you think is the best promise that God makes to God's people in this passage from Zephaniah?
✝ How important is God making promises to God's people? How important are God's promises to your faith?
✝ What does God promise us? What responsibilities come along with those promises? What must you promise God in return?

Learning to Trust

Say: "Through the angel Gabriel, God makes at least two promises, or assurances, to Mary in **Luke 1:26-38.** One is that Mary will have God's child. Another is that Mary has found favor with God. Though she probably finds the first promise intimidating, we know that Mary takes the second commandment to heart. She shows that she trusts God when she says, 'Here am I, the servant of the Lord; let it be with me according to your word.'

"Trust is one of the most important things that we as humans have to give and protect. But trust can also be difficult to build and is easily broken. This activity will help us learn to better trust one another."

Have your teens form one large circle. (If you have a large number of youth, form multiple circles.) Choose one person from the circle to be "it." Have the "it" person walk over to another member of the group, look the teen directly in the eye, and ask: "Can I trust you? Can I really, really trust you?" Instruct the person being addressed to respond by looking "it" directly in the eye and saying three times without laughing or giggling, "I promise you can trust me." If this person laughs or giggles, he or she becomes the new "it." If he or she can keep a straight face, the person who is "it" must repeat this process with someone else. (Unless you have few group members, tell the person who is "it" not to pick teens who have already been chosen.)

After everyone has had a chance to participate in the game at least once, say: "Trusting God is necessary for growing in faith. Learning to trust one another and taking care of the trust that others give us are necessary for building strong relationships. Take a moment to think of one way you can commit to strengthening your trust in God this Advent season." (You might have the youth write this commitment on a slip of paper they can keep in their wallet, purse, or Bible.)

Closing Prayer

Close your time together by praying the following prayer:

> *God of Hope and Promise,*
>
> *On behalf of your whole creation, you entrusted Mary with the great task of carrying and bearing your Son. Thank you for her faith in you and her willingness to trust your promises. Grant us to have faith like hers and to learn to love and trust you so that we may be ready and willing servants for your kingdom. In the name of Christ our Lord, amen.*

Notes

You Will Need
- slips of paper (optional)
- pens or pencils (optional)

Bible Study

Luke 1:5-9

You will need *paper, a pen or pencil, chalk or markers, scissors, and Bibles.*

Beforehand, duplicate this page and cut apart the letters to the right.

Say: "The first chapter of Luke's Gospel tells of the beginnings of not one but two miraculous lives. As we read from this chapter, think about the remarkable circumstances surrounding the births of these two remarkable people."

Distribute Bibles, and ask volunteers to read aloud **Luke 1:5-39** while the other youth follow along. Ask the youth these questions:

✝ What are the names of John's parents?
✝ What is John's father's occupation?
✝ Who brings the news that John will be born?
✝ How does John's father react to the news? What are the consequences of his reaction?
✝ Why, do you think, is John's father skeptical about the news that John will be born?
✝ Where does Mary, Jesus' mother, live?
✝ Who brings the news that Jesus will be born?
✝ What is Jesus' mother's reaction to the news?
✝ Describe the relationship between Jesus' and John's mothers.

Say: "You have probably read advice columns in newspapers or magazines in which anonymous people write letters to the columnist, explaining a problem or crisis in their lives. The columnist then responds with words of wisdom or suggestions to help the troubled reader."

In this exercise, the participants will become advice columnists. Requesting their advice are three characters from the Scripture lesson in Luke. Divide the youth into three groups; then give paper, pens or pencils, and one of the three letters to each group. And ask the teens to have a group member read aloud the letter and to write responses that address the person's spiritual and practical needs. (Allow each group to create a clever advice-columnist name for itself.)

Dear _____,

I am a priest in Judea. My wife and I are getting up there in years, but I have just gotten the unbelievable news that we are going to have a son! The trouble is, I didn't quite believe the angel who gave me the news, and he took away my voice until the day my son is born. How can I keep from losing my voice in the future, and how am I supposed to raise a son at my age?

Please help,
Silent Z

Dear _____,

I have a young relative who is unexpectedly pregnant. She says that she is still a virgin and that the baby is God's. She is an amazing girl but is worried, and I'm worried for her. I am also expecting a baby, but I'm older and better equipped to handle it. What should I say to help my young relative during this difficult time?

Let me know,
Concerned E

Dear _____,

I'm very young and have just learned that I'm pregnant with a son. I have it on good authority that he will be a special boy. The trouble is, I am not yet married to my fiancé, and I fear he'll think I've been unfaithful. I know this child was conceived by God, but I don't know how to tell my fiancé (or if he'll believe me). Can you help?

Anxious but brave,
Little M

Have each group present its response. (You might have computer-savvy youth create a newspaper-page display of the responses that you could hang in your meeting space.) Check on how the youth are doing with the Advent disciplines they began at week 1. Have a volunteer say a closing prayer.

Fourth Sunday

The Fourth Sunday of Advent

Key Verse: "Do not be afraid; for see—I am bringing you good news of great joy for all the people: to you is born this day in the city of David a Savior, who is the Messiah, the Lord" (**Luke 2:10b-11**).

Old Testament: **Isaiah 52:7-10**
("How beautiful . . . are the feet of the messenger who announces peace.")

New Testament: **Luke 2:1-20** (The story of Jesus' birth in Bethlehem)

When (and to Whom) God Arrives

Chances are, this Sunday will be your final meeting with your youth before you celebrate Christmas. Thus this session focuses on the story of Jesus' birth recorded in **Luke 2,** a reading most churches reserve for Christmas Eve or Christmas Day. The passage contains some of the most famous and memorable characters and images in the entire Bible.

Not every Gospel tells the nativity story as Luke does. Neither Mark nor John includes a birth narrative (though John gives a beautiful explanation of how Christ is eternally of and with God). The Gospels of Matthew and Luke, on the other hand, tell the story; but each incorporates different details into its telling of the event.

The popular versions of the Christmas story combine Matthew and Luke's accounts. Most nativity scenes feature Mary, Joseph, and baby Jesus surrounded by angels, animals, shepherds, and magi, or wise men. (See, for example, the Christmas play on pages 52–71.) The reality is that neither Gospel story puts them all at the scene at the same time. Only Luke mentions shepherds, who were present at the stable, while Matthew introduces the magi, who arrive much later (by which time, the shepherds would have presumably returned to their flocks). While some people are disillusioned to learn that the usual depiction of the manger scene is biblically inaccurate, clearing up the popular misconceptions gives us an opportunity to tell and hear the nativity story in powerful, new ways.

How do you bring Christ into the world?

Luke offers the most details about the event of Jesus' birth and gives us great insight into God's incarnation as that baby in Bethlehem. Some of Luke's information may seem boring or irrelevant. For example, he begins by naming the political leaders in power when Jesus was born (Caesar Augustus and Quirinius, a regional governor).

But this information about the government is more than a simple statement of fact. Luke announces the birth of Jesus, the Messiah, over and against the presence of imperial powers that ruled God's people. The people of Israel, and the people of the entire Mediterranean world, may have felt as though they were at the mercy of the Roman Empire and its provincial leaders; but Luke suggests that a new, greater power had arrived in the most unlikely of settings. Moreover, Roman civic religion held that Caesar Augustus was the divine son of a Roman god. Luke tells the story of a true divine Son who is nothing like the Roman emperor.

According to Luke's story, Jesus' parents could find no place to stay the night of Jesus' birth, and the Christ Child spent his first night in a feedbox for animals. The first people to hear of his birth were not nobles or rulers but shepherds working the graveyard shift. (Shepherding was not a highly regarded profession in ancient times. It was a dirty job, and shepherds had little political clout.) The angels' direct announcement to these lowly shepherds shows that God's arrival in Jesus Christ is good news for all people, including the economically poor and socially powerless. That the shepherds were the first to receive the message suggests that poor and seemingly unimportant people play vital roles in God's plan to redeem the world. (The magi in Matthew are important for other reasons, but this Sunday the focus is on the shepherds.)

Many youth can relate to those shepherds. Young people often feel powerless; some even feel invisible. And many teens have done "dirty work," whether it was yard work, babysitting young children bent on destruction, or pulling dinner shifts at a restaurant. The Christmas story affirms that these youth continue to play an important part in the story of God's saving grace.

This story also speaks to youthful ambition and idealism. God came into the world as a child born in the most humble of settings. A casual observer passing by the stable that evening may have felt pity, rather than hope, joy, or promise. What hope does a child have who is born in a feeding trough and whose only visitors are lowly shepherds? Not only did this child *have* hope—he *was* hope. The child in the stable, not the emperor in the palace, was the fulfillment of God's promise of justice and redemption.

Fourth Sunday

Mission Plan

Activity	Supplies
<u>Light the Fourth Advent Candle</u>	• Advent wreath • Bible • matches
<u>Getting the Whole Story</u>	• large writing surface • chalk or markers • Bibles • paper • pens or pencils
<u>Pondering in Your Heart</u>	• Bibles • paper • pens or pencils
<u>Beautiful Feet</u>	• Bibles • index cards • a pens or pencil
<u>Christmas Fever</u>	• copies of Christmas Fever! handout (page 50) • pens or pencils • small prize (optional)
<u>The Most Important Thing</u>	• paper • pens, pencils, or markers
<u>Closing Prayer</u>	No supplies needed

<u>Bible Study: Luke 2:1-20</u>

You will need Bibles, paper, and pens or pencils. Optional: a large writing surface and markers or chalk.

You Will Need
- Advent wreath
- Bible
- matches

*Adapted from *From Hope to Joy.*
Copyright © 1984 by Abingdon Press.
Used by permission.

You Will Need
- large writing surface
- chalk or markers
- Bibles
- paper
- pens or pencils

Light the Fourth Advent Candle

Begin this session by using the following short service:

1. Have a volunteer read aloud **Isaiah 9:6-7.**

2. Light the first, second, and third Advent candles.

3. Light the fourth candle. As the fourth candle is lighted, instruct a volunteer to read aloud:

> We light this candle as a symbol of the Prince of Peace.
> May the visitation of your Holy Spirit, O God,
> make us ready for the coming of Jesus, our hope and joy.
> O come, O come, Emmanuel.*

Getting the Whole Story

As the youth arrive, instruct them to write on a large writing surface every detail of the Christmas story that they can think of. When everyone has arrived and has had a chance to contribute, go through the list and have youth vote on whether they think each detail can be found in the Bible. Write *yes, no,* or *maybe* next to each item, based on how the majority of the youth vote. (Don't draw attention to who added a given item to the list.) If your youth have a strong knowledge of the Bible, have them vote on which Gospel contains certain details.

Say: "Many people know something about the Christmas story. Even those who have little knowledge of Christianity or Jesus' life are familiar with the major details of the Christmas story. But which of our ideas about the nativity story come from TV specials, Christmas plays, and nativity scenes, and which come from the Bible?"

Divide the teens into four groups, and distribute Bibles, paper, and pens or pencils. Assign each group a different Gospel. Tell the groups to find the story of Jesus' birth in their assigned Gospel and to list any details they feel are important to their Gospel's telling of the story. Have the groups select a spokesperson who will report to the rest of the youth.

The Mark and John groups will likely become frustrated because their Gospels contain no traditional nativity story. Challenge the John group to make the case that **John 1:1-18** is a birth story of a different kind. Ask the Mark group to discuss possible reasons why Mark did not include a birth narrative or why he started with John the Baptist.

Give the groups plenty of time to read and discuss. Then ask each group's spokesperson to report his or her group's findings. Refer the youth to your original list of Christmas-story details. (If the teens voted only on whether the details are found in Scripture, ask them to determine the answer to that question.) Note beside each detail which Gospel it is from.

Then ask:

✝ What surprised you in this activity?

✝ What details about the Christmas story had you gotten wrong?

Say: "The Christmas story is one of the most popular Christian stories, and it is also one of the stories most central to our faith. While telling this narrative in different ways is important, we always need to go back to the source, the Bible, and study the true version of the story."

Pondering in Your Heart

Say: "The Gospel of Luke was eloquently written and tells the stories of Jesus—including the story of his birth—in full and rich ways."

Invite a youth or an adult guest to read aloud **Luke 2:1-20** while the others follow along.

Then instruct the youth to silently reread verses 15-20. (You may wish to point out that Matthew's Gospel seldom mentions Jesus' mother in the birth story. Instead, Joseph, Mary's husband, is a primary character. However, in Luke much of the story focuses on Mary's participation in God's greatest act. Luke records her words, her reactions, and even her thoughts. She is a critical figure for anyone who wants to understand Luke's Gospel and the faith in Christ that the author commends.)

Point out that **Luke 2:19** says, "But Mary treasured all these words and pondered them in her heart." Say: "Luke portrays Mary as being calm and composed, especially for someone who has given birth under the circumstances she faced. But what do you think she pondered in her heart? For that matter, what were any of the characters in the story pondering in their hearts?"

Assign each youth one of the characters listed to the right. (It is OK if more than one youth are assigned the same character.)

If you have many youth, divide them into groups of teens that have the same character. Distribute paper and pens or pencils. Instruct each person (or group) to think about and write down what his or her respective character might have been pondering as the character participated in the event of Jesus' birth. Challenge the students to imagine what questions and thoughts their character might have had.

Give the youth plenty of time to work. Then have individuals or groups summarize their characters' thoughts and questions.

Finally, have the youth spend time individually writing what they ponder about Jesus, his birth, and what following him means. Allow volunteers to read what they have written.

You Will Need
• Bibles
• paper
• pens or pencils

Beforehand, invite a youth or an adult guest to read aloud Luke 2:1-20, and ask him or her to go over any strange pronunciations.

Characters
• Mary
• Joseph
• shepherds
• angels
• citizens of Bethlehem

Beforehand, divide Isaiah 52:7-10 into eight sections. (Each of the four verses naturally breaks into two parts, for a total of eight sections.) Write each section on a separate index card. Repeat this process until you have one set of cards for every three youth you expect. Shuffle each set of cards.

Option: Make this activity a competition, and award prizes to the first group to put the cards in the correct order.

Option: Repeat this activity with Luke 2:1-20. But instead of repeatedly reading the text aloud, challenge the youth to put the cards in order by memory.

You Will Need
- copies of Christmas Fever! handout (page 50)
- pens or pencils
- small prize (optional)

Beautiful Feet

Distribute the Bibles. Ask volunteers to read aloud **Isaiah 52:7-10,** with each person reading a verse at a time.

Say: "Feet are not the most appreciated parts of the human body. Consider all of the ways that we keep them from sight: We wear socks and cover them with shoes, we stand behind podiums, and we sit at tables. After all, these hard-working body parts get sweaty and sometimes smelly. Feet are rarely adored; some people are embarrassed to show their feet in public.

"Yet, Isaiah rejoiced in the feet of a messenger who announced, 'Your God reigns.' That feeling was present throughout the Christmas story in Luke as angels brought the news of Jesus' birth to shepherds, people who did not get much respect. Then the shepherds carried to Bethlehem the news of what they had seen. And their dusty, dirty feet became beautiful to anyone who would hear the amazing words that they had to share."

This exercise will give the participants not a hands-on but a feet-on experience of **Isaiah 52:7-10.** Collect the Bibles, and divide the youth into groups of three or four. Give each group a shuffled set of cards (see the margin), and have the groups scatter the cards on the floor in front of them. Instruct the groups to put the cards in order using only their feet. As the youth are working, read aloud **Isaiah 52:7-10** several times.

Christmas Fever!

Distribute copies of Christmas Fever! handout (page 50) and pens or pencils.

Ask the youth some questions about the Christmas story in **Luke 2:1-20** (such as the ones below). Include questions of varying levels of difficulty. For each one they answer correctly, they can move up one degree on their Christmas Fever! thermometer by shading one of the spaces. Declare the first person to answer nine questions the winner. (You may wish to give a small prize to the winner.)

Here are some questions you might ask (but feel free to come up with others on your own):

1. To whom was Mary engaged? (Joseph)

2. Which Roman emperor sent out the decree causing Mary and Joseph to go to Bethlehem? (Augustus)

3. True, or false: **Luke 2** says that Mary rode into Bethlehem on a borrowed donkey. (false)

4. How did the angel identify Bethlehem to the shepherds? (as the City of David)

5. How many magi or wisemen does Luke say went to visit Jesus after he was born? (Trick question—Luke does not mention magi.)

6. Where does Luke say the angels went after they told the good news to the shepherds? (into heaven)

7. Luke reports that the shepherds found the baby Jesus lying in _____. (a manger)

8. The angels in the story described what they had to tell the shepherds as "good news of great _____." (joy)

9. True, or False: Luke says the shepherds were pretty disappointed by what they found in Bethlehem. (false)

10. Who is the governor of Syria at the time of Jesus' birth? (Quirinius)

11. True, or false: Luke says that the shepherds were, at first, frightened by the angels. (true)

12. Why did Mary and Joseph have to go to Bethlehem to register? (Every man was required to go to the home of his ancestors, and Joseph's ancestor, David, was from Bethlehem.)

The Most Important Thing

Invite the students to read silently **Luke 2:1-20** one more time. Then invite the youth to reflect on this question: What is the most important thing I can tell others about the story of Jesus' birth?

Hand out paper and pens, pencils, or markers, and allow the youth time to write or draw their response to that question. Then invite the teens to read or show what they have done.

Closing Prayer

Close your time together with the following prayer.

Almighty God,

In your greatness and humility, you chose to become like one of us. You surprised Mary and Joseph. You surprised the shepherds. And you continue to surprise us with the ways in which you bless us. Help us to continue being heralds of the good news the angels proclaimed in Bethlehem so long ago. And let us ponder your wondrous love always in our hearts. Amen.

You Will Need
- paper
- pens, pencils, or markers

Option: If the youth are willing, work with them to post their responses on a church website or to print them in a bulletin or newsletter.

Bible Study

Luke 2:1-20

You will need *Bibles, paper, and pens or pencils. Optional: a large writing surface and markers or chalk.*

Sometimes teens experience a Scripture most vividly when they imagine themselves as part of the story. This study will enable the youth to focus their imaginative energies on better understanding Luke's account of Jesus' birth.

Begin by distributing the Bibles. Have the youth read aloud **Luke 2:1-20,** with each youth reading a verse at a time. Then explain to the teens that they will hear the story again several times and that they are going to be a part of it.

Hand out paper and pens or pencils, but tell the youth not to write anything yet. Assign each students one of the characters listed below. Instruct the students to imagine themselves as their character as you read aloud **Luke 2:1-20.** (Not all of the characters to whom the youth are assigned appear explicitly in Luke's story. Some are assumed to be behind-the-scenes figures who might have an interesting perspective.)

Characters:
- Mary
- Joseph
- baby Jesus
- a shepherd
- an angel
- the innkeeper
- an animal in the stable
- a guest at the inn
- one of the shepherds' sheep
- a traveler on the road to Bethlehem

When you have finished reading, instruct the youth to write down answers to the following questions, which you might write on a large writing surface:*

✝ What did you see?

✝ Who was there?

✝ What smells or tastes did you experience?

✝ What sounds did you hear?

✝ What decisions did you have to make, or what decisions will you have to make?

✝ How did you feel as you watched everything happening?

✝ What would you like to say to the other people at the stable witnessing the nativity?

✝ What should you do next?

✝ What does your experience tell you about God? How has it affected your relationship with God?

✝ What about your experience do you most want to tell others?

*Option: Instead of having the youth write down their answers, assign pairs or have the teens pair off, and ask the youth to discuss their answers with their partner.

Read the Scripture several times. Each time, have the youth imagine themselves as a different character. At the end, ask:

✝ What new insight have you gained through this activity?

✝ Which character did you find most interesting to imagine yourself as?

✝ Which character can you most relate to? Why?

✝ How might this exercise affect how you tell the story of Jesus' birth?

Close your session by praying and by checking on how the youth are keeping up with their prayers for a group member that they began on the first Sunday of Advent.

Sunday After

The Sunday After Christmas

Key Verse: "At that moment [Anna] came, and began to praise God and to speak about the child to all who were looking for the redemption of Jerusalem" (**Luke 2:38**).

Old Testament: Isaiah **61:10—62:3** ("I will greatly rejoice in the LORD.")

New Testament: Luke 2:21-40 (Jesus is presented in the Temple.)

Only the Beginning

The season of Advent is more than just four weeks leading up to Christmas. Advent is a time of grace when God beckons all Christians to prepare themselves for Christ's arrival, and it begins another year of celebrating God's love for creation.

If Advent is more than a prelude to Christmas, then Christmas is much more than a one-day celebration—it is a season all its own. Christmas starts with the baby born in the manger but also includes the Bible's few stories about Jesus' childhood and youth. The Gospels tell of exotic visitors bringing gifts to Jesus and of threats to his life almost as soon as it begins.

From his birth, we know that Jesus' life will be unique. His radical teaching, miracles, way with people, unjust death, and glorious resurrection bear this truth out. In **Luke 2:25-38,** the prophetic voices of two characters named Simeon and Anna proclaim thanks to God for Jesus' extraordinary existence and all that lies ahead for him.

Simeon and Anna also speak of the promise and significance of a life lived in conjunction with God's will. Jesus echoes this promise in his adult ministry, as he teaches about the kingdom of God and the need for repentance. Simeon, Anna, and Jesus alike remind us that a life dedicated to God and open to God's purposes will be a full life. Of course, neither Jesus nor the prophets who come before him suggest that a life devoted to God will be easy. Rich and meaningful, yes; a cakewalk, no.

Notice what Simeon says to Mary as he concludes his blessing of the baby Jesus: "This child is destined for the falling and rising of many in Israel, and to be a sign that will be opposed so that the inner thoughts of many will be revealed—and a sword will pierce your own soul too" (**Luke 34b-35**). This statement predicts a life that will have far-reaching effects. At the same time, Anna praises God for the child, who will be the redemption of Israel. Anna and Simeon have lofty expectations for someone so young.

How have you dedicated your life to God?

Yet, God has lofty expectations for all young people. Each student you teach is starting or continuing a journey of faith that will affect not only him or her but potentially thousands of others. As Advent prepares us for Christmas, adolescence prepares us for a mature life of faith lived according to God's promises.

After a month of intense preparation, making it to Christmas might feel like reaching a destination. But Christmas is more of a beginning than a conclusion. So are many milestones in the lives of young Christians. Youth prepare for confirmation, graduation, and adulthood. At times, the preparation is grueling. Still, each of these milestones is a starting point, and the journey ahead is full of promise.

Sunday After

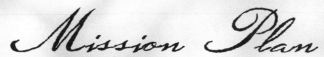
Mission Plan

Activity	Supplies
<u>Light the Christmas Candle</u>	• Advent wreath • Bible • matches
<u>Holy to the Lord</u>	• paper • pens or pencils • large writing surface • marker or piece of chalk • Bible
<u>A Promise Kept</u>	• copies of A Promise Kept handout (page 51) • scissors • pens or pencils • blank adhesive labels, business cards, or index cards
<u>Praise Circle</u>	• Bible
<u>Rejoice in the Lord</u>	• Bible
<u>A Christmas Acrostic</u>	• copies of A Christmas Acrostic handout (page 51)
<u>Lord, Dismiss Your Servants</u>	No supplies needed

<u>Bible Study: Luke 2:21-40</u>

You will need Bibles and copies of the Bible Dictionary (pages 78–80).
Optional: other Bible dictionaries and concordances.

Light the Christmas Candle

Begin this session by lighting the first four Advent candles and the Christmas candle using the following short service:

1. Have a volunteer read **Isaiah 9:2-7.**

2. Light the Advent candles and the central Christ candle.

3. Have a volunteer say: "We light this candle as a symbol of the arrival of the Light of the World. The people who walked in darkness have seen a great light. We give thanks for you, O Emmanuel, for God is with us."

Holy to the Lord

Say: "Luke tells us that Jesus' parents followed the accepted religious practice of observant Jews in his day. When Jesus was eight days old, his parents took him to be circumcised and officially named. He was also taken to the Temple in Jerusalem to be presented to God, because the law of Moses says, 'Every firstborn male shall be designated as holy to the Lord' (**Luke 2:23b**).

"In the church today, people talk about holiness. Though religious leaders use the word in different ways, holiness is the quality of belonging to or being of God. Being holy means being dedicated solely to God."

Hand out paper and pens or pencils, and write the following questions on a large writing surface:

✞ What does it mean for something to be holy?

✞ What are some things you think are holy?

✞ What in your life would you consider holy?

Instruct the youth to write or draw a response to each question. Some youth might be intimidated by the idea of holiness, fearing that they never live up to their notion of being holy. Others may simply consider holiness no fun. Stress that holiness is foremost about having a lively and meaningful relationship with God. Challenge the teens to think "outside the church building" in responding to these questions.

After giving the youth a few minutes to work, invite volunteers to read or present some of their answers. Then say: "Holiness is an important part of any Christian's life and faith. Being holy does not mean never sinning or spending all of our spare time at the church. It does mean reminding ourselves that we are children of God and disciples of Christ and allowing this truth to affect our attitudes and behaviors and to transform our hearts."

Ask a volunteer to read aloud **Exodus 13:1-2,** a source of the command Mary and Joseph were following by taking Jesus to Jerusalem, according to Luke. Tell the youth that regardless of whether they are firstborn, God considers them blessed children. Then ask them to complete on paper the following sentences:

✝ I can express holiness in my life by . . .

✝ Something in my life that I can dedicate to God is . . .

Allow volunteers to relay their responses. Encourage all of the youth to keep their sheets of paper and continue thinking of ways they can dedicate their lives to God.

A Promise Kept

Say: "Simeon's story in **Luke 2** is touching. God fulfilled the Holy Spirit's revelation to Simeon that he would not die until he had seen the one who would redeem God's people. The old, devout man finally laid eyes on Jesus, God's promised Savior. Then Simeon offered prophetic words of promise for the child, for Israel, and for the world. But what truly stands out in this Scripture is the promise God kept to Simeon. And when Simeon saw the infant Jesus, he broke out in praise and thanksgiving, celebrating God's faithfulness not only to him but to all of God's people."

Divide the youth into groups of three or four, and distribute pens or pencils and copies of A Promise Kept handout (page 51). Instruct each group to work together to complete the statements on the handout (which are listed below).

✝ We can always count on God to _____.

✝ We know that God will never _____.

✝ We believe that God will keep God's promise to _____ _____.

✝ God's promises inspire us to _____.

✝ A promise we will keep to God is _____ _____.

Allow the youth plenty of time to work, then have a representative from each group read aloud his or her group's answers.

Next, distribute the blank cards or adhesive labels, and instruct each youth to write on the card or label a promise to God he or she will make and keep. Encourage the students to place the card in their

You Will Need
- copies of A Promise Kept handout (page 51)
- scissors
- pens or pencils
- blank adhesive labels, business cards, or index cards

Beforehand, cut the handout in half, along the dotted lines.

Note: Youth need to know that they can trust God. Many teens have been disappointed by empty promises. They may have been let down by friends, adults, or even parents. Simeon's story offers assurance that God keeps God's promises.

At the same time, youth can easily confuse requests they hope God will fulfill with biblical promises God endorses. For example, God promises in the Bible that we are never beyond God's grace. Rewarding someone with a new car if he or she goes to church every Sunday for a year, on the other hand, is not the type of promise God tends to make.

purses or wallets or to stick the label on a folder or somewhere in their room where they will see it, so that they will often be reminded of their promise to God.

Praise Circle

Say: "Another prominent character in the story of Jesus' presentation in the Temple in Jerusalem is the prophet Anna. Like Simeon, she had been waiting a long time to see the fulfillment of God's plan to redeem God's people." Ask a volunteer to read aloud **Luke 2:36-38.**

Say: "For many of us, the Christmas season often stirs up good feelings. It reminds us of God's faithfulness and graciousness. And since Christmas is near the beginning of the Christian year, it is an excellent time to get in the habit of praising and thanking God for all of the blessings in our lives, a practice that people of faith too often neglect."

Instruct the youth to sit in a circle. (If you have many students, have them form multiple circles, with no more than ten youth in any circle.) Ask for a volunteer to begin the praise circle. Starting with this volunteer and going around the circle, instruct the participants to shout out praises to God (such as, "Thank God for . . . " and "Praise God for . . . "). Encourage enthusiasm, and tell the youth not to repeat praises.

Option: Do this exercise several times, and see how quickly the youth can go around the circle without repeating what anyone says.

Rejoice in the Lord

Hand out the Bibles, and ask the youth to turn to **Isaiah 61:10–62:3.** Ask volunteers to each read aloud a few verses while the others follow along. Then ask the following questions:

✞ Why, do you think, is this passage appropriate to read during the Christmas season?

✞ In what ways have you seen "righteousness and praise spring up" (**Isaiah 61:11**) during this year's Advent and Christmas seasons?

✞ How do you envision "garments of salvation" (**Isaiah 61:10**)?

✞ When have you wanted something so much that you would not rest or keep silent until it became a reality?

✞ In what ways do you see God's salvation in the world?

✞ In what ways do you see God's salvation as yet to arrive?

✞ How can you, your youth group, or your congregation be "a crown of beauty in the hand of the Lord" (**Isaiah 62:3**)?

You Will Need
• Bible

You Will Need
• Bibles

You Will Need
- copies of A Christmas Acrostic handout (page 51)
- pens or pencils
- large writing surface (optional)
- chalk or markers (optional)

If you have not done the activity A Promise Kept, cut A Christmas Acrostic handout (page 51) apart from A Promise Kept handout (page 51).

Say: "Jesus' birth began God's salvation and redemption in the world. Because of Jesus's death and resurrection, each of us can be forgiven of our sins and restore our relationship with God. But we also have a role to play in the story of God's salvation. We are called not to keep silent and rest, as we spread the good news of Christ through our words, actions, and attitudes."

A Christmas Acrostic

Say: "We have spent the past four weeks preparing for Christmas and God's greatest gift. Now it's time to thank and praise God for the wonderful gift of Jesus Christ. We can praise and thank God in many ways—through our prayers and worship and through our service and actions."

Distribute copies of A Christmas Acrostic handout (page 51) and pens or pencils. Instruct the youth to create an acrostic poem that expresses joy and gratitude for God's gift of Christ. An acrostic is simply a poem that spells out a word by having each line begin with a letter of that word. For instance, an acrostic poem for the word *Lord* would be

> **L**oving
> **O**verwhelming
> **R**ighteous
> **D**ivine

Give the youth ample time to complete their acrostics, and create one of your own. Then allow volunteers to read what they have created, and read your poem to the youth. If time permits, work together to create a composite Christmas acrostic for the entire group, using a large writing surface and chalk or markers.

Lord, Dismiss Your Servants

Close your time together by turning back to Simeon's words in **Luke 2:29-33.** The *Nunc Dimittis* (also known as the "Canticle of Simeon") is a traditional benediction used in many Christian traditions. Pray this ancient prayer to conclude your time together during these holy seasons:

> *Lord, now let your servant go in peace:*
> *your word has been fulfilled.*
> *My own eyes have seen the salvation*
> *which you have prepared in the presence of every people:*
> *a light to reveal you to the nations*
> *and the glory of your people Israel.**

*English translation of the *Nunc Dimittis* copyright © 1988, by the English Language Liturgical Consultation. Used by permission.

Bible Study

Luke 2:21-40

You will need Bibles, paper, pens or pencils, copies of the Bible Dictionary (pages 78–80), one small votive candle, a small cross, one large Christ candle, and matches.

Ask:

✝ What rituals and traditions have you participated in that identify you as a child of God? (Answers may include baptism, Holy Communion, confirmation, and lighting the Advent candles.)

✝ Why, do you think, are these rituals and traditions so important to Christians?

Say: "Though Jesus was God's Son, he did not consider himself above the rituals and traditions of his faith. He was baptized, participated in religious festivals, and made pilgrimages to the Temple in Jerusalem. And, keeping with Jewish custom, Jesus was circumcised and presented at the Temple when he was an infant. Jesus was unique—he was the Messiah and God in human form. But in some ways, Jesus was just one of God's many beloved children."

Ask volunteers to read aloud **Luke 2:21-40.** As they read the Scripture, instruct the youth to think about which character they most relate to. You might distribute small sheets of paper and have the teens jot down some notes about the character they choose and why they identify with him or her. For example, the students might relate to Anna because they see themselves as devoted to God and eager to give thanks for what God has given them. Or they might relate to Joseph and Mary (who are silent in this passage), because the youth feel they must take on a great responsibility.

After reading the Scripture, give the group members a few minutes to reflect on the character they have chosen. Then have the youth pair off and discuss their reflections with a partner.

Next, divide the youth into teams of three and five. Say, "All of the characters in this story are faithful to God." Instruct the teams to go through the Scripture and list ways in which the characters in this story—Simeon, Anna, Mary, and Joseph—are faithful. Distribute the Bible Dictionary on pages 78–80, in case the youth need to refer to it. Give the teams plenty of time to work; then compile a group list on a large writing surface. Here are some examples of responses:

✝ Mary and Joseph were true to Jewish law by presenting Jesus, their firstborn male.

✝ Simeon was righteous man who trusted the Holy Spirit and eagerly awaited the Messiah.

Say: "Faithfulness is a constant theme throughout the Bible. God's hope is that we will choose to be faithful in response to God's fidelity towards us. For many of us—like Jesus—a life of faithfulness begins when our parents, families, and church families dedicate us to God through baptism, teaching us about the faith, and involving us in the life of the church."

Give the youth an opportunity to express their desire and willingness to live a life of faithfulness to God. Distribute small votive candles. At the front of your youth room, set up a small cross on a table, and light one tall white candle (or use the Christ candle from your Advent wreath). Light this tall candle.

Ask the class to sing a familiar hymn or song of praise, such as "This Little Light of Mine." As they sing, encourage the youth to offer a prayer to God in which they commit themselves to living as faithful Christians throughout the entire year. After they pray silently or as they pray, invite the teens to light their votive candles from the Christ candle and set them on the table.

Close the Bible study with a prayer of thanks to God for your time together.

Signs of the (Advent) Season

Different sectors of society mark the Advent season in various ways. In the appropriate quadrant below, list what each sector of society does to get ready for Christmas.

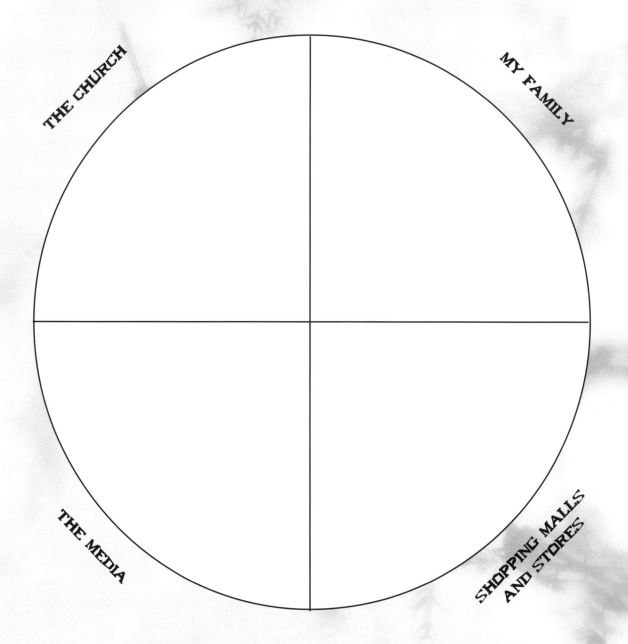

THE CHURCH

MY FAMILY

THE MEDIA

SHOPPING MALLS AND STORES

Impossible...
or Maybe Not

In the space below, list some things you think the world would have thought was impossible at the corresponding time in history.

2000 YEARS AGO,
PEOPLE WOULD HAVE THOUGHT THE FOLLOWING THINGS WERE IMPOSSIBLE:

500 YEARS AGO,
PEOPLE WOULD HAVE THOUGHT THE FOLLOWING THINGS WERE IMPOSSIBLE:

150 YEARS AGO,
PEOPLE WOULD HAVE THOUGHT THE FOLLOWING THINGS WERE IMPOSSIBLE:

50 YEARS AGO,
PEOPLE WOULD HAVE THOUGHT THE FOLLOWING THINGS WERE IMPOSSIBLE:

5 YEARS AGO,
PEOPLE THOUGHT THE FOLLOWING THINGS WERE IMPOSSIBLE:

RIGHT NOW,
PEOPLE THINK THE FOLLOWING THINGS ARE IMPOSSIBLE:

Prepare to Worship

Our Service of Advent Worship

Musical Prelude: _____

Opening Prayer: _____

_____

_____

_____

_____

Opening Hymn: _____

Prayer of Confession:_____

_____

_____

_____

_____

_____

_____

Light the Advent Wreath

Prepare to Worship
(Continued)

Scripture Lesson(s): _____

_____

Affirmation of Faith: _____

Prayers of the People and the Lord's Prayer

Offertory Hymn: _____

Prayer of Thanksgiving: _____

_____

_____

_____

Closing Hymn: _____

Benediction: _____

_____

_____

Christmas fever!

An angel of the Lord

The star of Bethlehem

A shepherd at the stable

Feeling jolly

Putting up the decorations

A little Christmas spirit

Bah, humbug!

Coal in your stocking

A Promise Kept

- We can always count on God to _____
_____ .

- We know that God will never _____ .

- We believe that God will keep God's promise to _____
_____ .

- God's promises inspire us to _____
_____ .

- A promise we will keep to God is _____
_____ .

- ✂

A Christmas Acrostic

An acrostic is a poem that spells out a word by beginning each line with a letter of that word. Create an acrostic to sum up what you have experienced and learned during Advent and Christmas.

C _____

H _____

R _____

I _____

S _____

T _____

M _____

A _____

S _____

What If...?

A Christmas Play for Youth*

Notes

CHARACTERS

Youth Leader	Shepherd 1
Mary	Shepherd 2
Joseph	Shepherd 3
Mary's Mother	Sheep Dog
Joseph's friend 1	Wise Person
Joseph's friend 2	King
Angel	Astrologer
Donkey Front	Camel
Donkey Back	Sheep Owner
Innkeeper	

SCENE 1

A youth group is gathered to talk about Christmas. The youth are dressed in normal attire for a youth meeting.

Youth Leader: OK. Listen to the story one more time. Luke 2:1-20: "In those days a decree went out from Emperor Augustus that all the world should be registered. This was the first registration and was taken while . . ." while kwa-RINE . . . um, while kwee-NIR . . . I mean, while kwigh-RIN-ee-us "was governor of Syria . . ."

Group yawns, stretches, moves around, talks, and so on.

Youth Leader: All right, I guess you have heard this all before. So, let's try something else. I want you to close your eyes. . . . Close your eyes! Now I want you to imagine the story and figure out whom you would like to be if you could become a part of the story.

Mary: I want to be Mary.

Joseph: Well, then I guess I will be Joseph.

Donkey Front: I wanted to be Mary.

*Play written by Steve Butler. Copyright © 2004 by Stephen H. Butler. All rights reserved. Used by permission.

Donkey Back: And I was going to be Joseph.

Youth Leader: Don't worry. There are plenty of parts for everyone.

King: Is someone supposed to be kwin . . . TIR-ee-us?

Wise Person: Well, I want to be a wise man.

King: Being a king would be cool.

Camel: Yeah, and so would hanging around the wise men.

Astrologer: It's *magi,* you clowns.

King: What's a magi?

Astrologer: A wise person.

Wise Person: That's what I am.

King: If you're so wise, why did you say "wise man" instead of "magician"?

Astrologer: Magi, not magician.

Camel: What's the difference?

Youth Leader: All right, magi, king, wise person, astrologer, they were called different things. *(To King, Wise Person, and Astrologer.)* Whatever they were, you three are they. You can figure out what to call yourselves. *(To Camel.)* And you can be their camel. *(To the shepherds.)* What about you guys?

Shepherd 1: I guess I'd be a shepherd, dude. I mean, how hard could that be?

Shepherd 2: Yeah, sitting around, watching sheep, playing with a dog.

Shepherd 3: Getting a tan.

Dog: I don't know. All those sheep—that's a lot of responsibility. I don't want to be a shepherd, but working with the shepherds might be nice.

Angel: Well, I would want to see it all. How can I do that?

Youth Leader: You could be an angel.

Angel: OK, that fits my personality, anyway.

The group jeers and groans.

Youth Leader: All right, *(to Innkeeper)* that leaves you.

Innkeeper: I don't know.

Leader: Why don't you be the innkeeper?

Innkeeper: I don't really want to be a mean person.

Youth Leader: Actually . . . if you think about it . . . the innkeeper was a nice person—a person who found a warm, safe place for Mary and Joseph.

Innkeeper: Well . . .

Youth Leader: That settles it; you're the innkeeper.

Angel: What about the people who aren't here?

Leader: Oh, I think we can come up with some other parts for them.

SCENE 2

From this point on, the youth are in costume as their respective characters.

Mary *enters and appears to be engaged in some task.* **Angel** *enters. She screams.*

Angel: Do not be afraid!

 Mary *screams.*

Angel: I said don't be afraid! I bring you good news!

Mary: What is this good news?

Angel: You have been chosen!

Mary: Chosen? Chosen for what?

Angel: You will give birth to a son, the Son of God, the Messiah.

Mary: Huh?

Angel: OK, I'll try to explain it as best I can: You're pregnant.

 Mary *screams.* **Mary** *and* **Angel** *exit.*

SCENE 3

King, Wise Person, Astrologer, *and* **Camel** *enter.*

King: You're a camel.

Camel: Bwaw.

King: Hey, guys, look, [name of actor]'s a camel.

Camel: Bwaw.

King: I guess this means I can ride [him or her].

Camel: Bwaw. *(He or she spits on King.)*

King: *(He wipes his face.)* Or I can just walk beside him.

Astrologer: Come on, we have a long way to go.

SCENE 4

Mother *enters.* **Mary** *enters and turns to her mother.*

Mary: Mom, I have something to tell you.

Mother: What is it, dear?

Mary: Mom, I'm pregnant.

Mother: Ooh! Just wait till your dad gets hold of that Joseph.

Mary: Mom, it's not Joe's baby.

Mother: *(She screams.)* OK, let's not panic. We can send you to my sister's place. You can hide there. *(Under her breath.)* And maybe your aunt can straighten you out.

Mary: Mom, wait.

Mother: You're right. There are things to do first. Who is it? Your father will take care of him. *(Under her breath.)* And in the meantime, I'll take care of you.

Mary: Mom, you don't understand. I'm still a virgin.

Mary *and* **Mother** *exit.*

SCENE 5

Joseph, Friend 1, *and* **Friend 2** *enter.*

Friend 1: Joe, you dog you!

Joseph: Huh?

Friend 2: You just couldn't wait.

Joseph: What are you talking about?

Friend 1: We're talking about you and Mary.

Joseph: Yeah, what about us?

Friend 2: What about?! About Mary being pregnant.

Joseph: What?!

Friend 2: Pregnant, you know, heavy with child, in maternal mode . . .

Joseph: *(Advancing on Friend 2 and making a fist.)* Take that back.

Friend 2: It's true. *(To Friend 1.)* Tell him.

Friend 1: It is true. But you don't know anything about it? Are you saying it's not yours?

Joseph: There's no way it could be mine. What should I do?

Friend 1: Ooh. I don't know. I'm sorry, man.

Friend 2: So am I. That's rough. But there is a bright side.

Friend 1: Bright side?

Friend 2: Yeah, we get to have a stoning. We haven't had a good stoning around here in ages.

Friend 1: You jerk! This is no time to talk about stoning his girlfriend! Can't you see he's really hurting here?

Friend 2: Well, throwing that first stone will cheer him up.

Joseph: There will be no stoning.

Friend 2: Awww. Then what are you going to do?

Joseph: I'm not sure; but there will be no stoning. Now, go away and leave me alone.

Friend 1 *and* **Friend 2** *exit.*

Angel *enters.* **Joseph** *screams.*

Angel: Do not be afraid.

Joseph: What do you want with me?

Angel: I am here to talk to you about Mary.

Joseph: What about Mary? Are you going to tell me that I have to obey the law and have her stoned?

Angel: No, I am here to tell you to marry her.

Joseph: I can't marry Mary. *(He chuckles. Under his breath.)* "Marry Mary." *(In a normal voice.)* I can't marry Mary. She's having someone else's baby.

Angel: Yes, she is. She is having God's baby.

Joseph: Say what?

Angel: Really, she is going to give birth to the Son of God. And you are going to marry her.

Joseph: Great. All these years of going to synagogue, and God does this to me!

Angel: Joseph, raising God's Son is a great blessing.

Joseph: OK, look. I've had a long day, and I'm not in the mood for jokes.

Angel: No joke, Joe. Mary is going to give birth to the Messiah. And you *will* marry her, because you are of the house and lineage of David. Now, we can do this the easy way, or we can do it the hard way.

Joseph: All right, all right, there's no need to get nasty.

Lights go down. **Joseph** *and* **Angel** *exit.*

SCENE 6

Youth Leader *enters.*

Youth Leader: Now a decree went out from Caesar Augustus that everyone must go to their home towns and be registered for the tax rolls. So Joseph took Mary, his wife, and went to Bethlehem, because he was from the house and family of David.

Lights come up.

Joseph *enters, leading the* **Donkey Front** *and* **Donkey Back. Mary** *has a protruding belly.*

Donkey Front: I'm the front of a donkey. I wanted to be Mary, and I'm the front of a donkey!

Donkey Back: Don't complain.

Joseph: Are you all right, dear?

Mary: I'm fine, just a little tired.

Mary *pauses and gets a startled look on her face.*

Mary: Joseph, honey, how long before we get to Bethlehem?

Joseph: I don't know for sure. It shouldn't be too long. Why?

Mary: I think my water just broke.

Donkey Back: Ewwwww.

All exit.

SCENE 7

Enter **Wise Person, King, Astrologer,** *and* **Camel.**

King: Are we there yet?

Wise Person: No.

King: Well, how long is it going to be?

Astrologer: I don't know for sure.

King: Guess.

Astrologer: OK. I guess one year, three months, seventeen days, and five hours.

Wise Person: Oh, thank you, Mr. Spock.

King: My feet are tired; I want to ride. *(Looks at Camel.)*

   Camel *spits in King's face.*

King: *(He wipes his face.)* Or not.

   All exit.

                    SCENE 8

Enter **Joseph, Mary, Donkey Front, Donkey Back,** *and* **Innkeeper. Mary** *is riding the donkey.*

Joseph: *(Knocking on door.)* Help, please. Open the door.

Innkeeper: *(Talking through the door.)* Go away. We don't have any more rooms.

Joseph: Well, we have a real problem here. My wife is about to have a baby.

Innkeeper: Real sorry about that. But there is really isn't much I can do. I don't have any room.

Joseph: I made a reservation.

Innkeeper: Sure. But look at the time. I can't wait forever. I'm running a business here. I had to give your room to someone who was actually here.

Mary: *(Groaning.)* Ohhhh.

Joseph: *(To himself.)* What am I going to do?

Innkeeper: Well, let's see. . . . I could let you stay in the stable. But that's the best I can do. It's dry. I just put down fresh hay this morning.

Donkey Front: Mmmmm. Hayyyyyy.

Donkey Rear: Don't even think about it.

Joseph: A stable? Mary, what do you think?

Mary: Take it. Take anything. Just get me off this donkey so that I can lie down.

Donkey Rear: Thank you, thank you, thank you.

Joseph: OK, we'll take it. But I want a discount.

Innkeeper: Sure. Just follow me.

All exit.

SCENE 9

Enter **Shepherds 1, 2,** *and* **3; Sheep Dog;** *and* **Sheep Owner.**

Sheep Owner: Shepherds, get over here. *(He pauses while the shepherds walk toward him.)* OK. I want to make sure you know what your job is.

Shepherd 1: We know already.

Shepherd 2: Yeah, we take the sheep up to pasture and watch them.

Shepherd 3: Pretty simple. We figure to catch some rays, work on the tan, write poetry and songs.

Sheep Owner: You idiots! That isn't what you do.

Shepherds: It's not?

Sheep Owner: No, you clowns. Let me ask you: What would you do if a lion were to come around looking for a nice leg of lamb for dinner?

Shepherd 1: Run.

Shepherd 2: Hide.

Shepherd 3: Yell.

Sheep Dog: GRRRRRR!

Sheep Owner: Well, at least one of you got it right. *(To the dog.)* Good [boy or girl]. *(To the shepherds.)* This is what you do: First, get between the lion and the sheep. Second, throw stones at the lion. This will cause the lion to either run away or get really angry. If it runs away, good job, well done, and all that. If it gets angry, stay between the lion and the sheep.

Shepherd 1: What happens then?

Sheep Owner: The lion doesn't eat the sheep.

Shepherd 2: Why not?

Sheep Owner: Because it will be full.

Shepherd 3: I don't like where this is going.

Sheep Owner: Well, boys, have fun with the sheep.

    Sheep Owner *exits.*

Shepherd 1: I don't want to be a shepherd anymore.

Shepherd 2: Neither do I.

Shepherd 3: Right, let's get out of here.

Sheep Dog: GRRRRR.

Shepherd 2: This dog doesn't look too friendly.

Shepherd 3: I don't think [he or she] is going to let us go.

Shepherd 1: OK, off to the pastures.

    Sheep Dog *barks and herds the shepherds off the stage.*

SCENE 10

Enter **Wise Person, King, Astrologer,** *and* **Camel.**

King: Are we there yet?

Wise Person, Astrologer: NO!

King: Well, how much further?

Wise Person: Why don't we change the subject? *(To the King.)* What did you bring as a gift?

King: Gold. You can't go wrong with gold. Everybody can always use a little extra gold. *(To Wise Person.)* What about you?

Wise Person: Frankincense.

King: What is that?

Wise Person: Incense. You burn it as an offering to God.

King: Oh, well, I guess that makes sense. *(He pauses. To Astrologer.)* Well, what about you?

Astrologer: It's a surprise.

King: Come on, we've told you what we've brought.

Wise Person: Yeah, come on, give it up.

Astrologer: Myrrh.

King: What?

Wise Person: You're kidding.

Astrologer: No.

King: What is myrrh?

Wise Person: You better tell him.

Astrologer: OK. Myrrh is an aromatic resin used in the process of embalming a dead person.

Camel: Bwawawaw!

King: Yeck! You're giving that to a baby?

Astrologer: Look, it's what the stars said I should bring. What could I do?

King: Bring something nice, like gold.

Wise Person, Astrologer, King, *and* **Camel** *exit.*

SCENE 11

Enter **Shepherds 1, 2,** *and* **3** *and* **Sheep Dog.**

Shepherd 1: Did you hear that?

Shepherd 2: What?

Shepherd 3: I didn't hear anything.

Shepherd 1: I thought I heard a howl, like a wolf.

Shepherd 2: Don't mess around, dude.

Shepherd 3: This job is bad enough without you hearing things that aren't there.

Sheep Dog: *(Sneaks up behind Shepherd 1.)* Ah-oooooo!

Shepherd 2: *(To Sheep Dog.)* Don't you start.

Shepherd 3: It's been a long and miserable day. I'm cold, hungry, and tired. I'm going to bed.

Shepherd 1: Sounds good.

Shepherd 2: Who's going to watch the flocks by night?

Shepherd 1: The dog can.

Shepherd 3: Yeah, [he or she]'s better at this than we are, anyway.

Shepherd 2: Plus, [he or she]'d be faster than we'd be if a wolf came around.

Shepherd 1: All right, dog, watch the sheep, and don't let anything eat them.

Sheep Dog: Grrrrrr.

    Shepherds 1, 2, *and* **3** *lie down to sleep.* **Angel** *enters.*

Sheep Dog: *(Trying to hide.)* Arf, arf, arf.

Angel: OK, I've just about had it. Why does everyone scream or hide or something whenever I appear?

    Youth Leader *enters.*

Youth Leader: Well, you are an angel.

Angel: Yeah, so what? I'm one of the good guys.

Youth Leader: True. But think of it this way: How often does the average person see an angel?

Angel: I don't get it.

Youth Leader: OK, look at it another way: Some people back then expected that God would send the angels as God's army . . . when the world ended.

Angel: Ohhhh.

Youth Leader: Now do you understand why you have to tell everyone not to be afraid?

Angel: Yeah, I guess so.

Youth Leader: OK. I guess I'll let you get back to work.

Youth Leader *exits.*

Angel: *(To the dog.)* Here, [boy or girl], come on, [girl or boy], don't be afraid.

Sheep Dog *walks toward the angel.*

Angel: That's a good dog. Now, wake up your masters.

Sheep Dog *walks over to the shepherds, bats them with his or her paw, and barks several times.*

Shepherd 1: *(Awakening.)* What is it, [boy or girl]? Is Timmy in trouble?

Sheep Dog *barks several times.* **Shepherd 1** *notices the angel and screams.*

Shepherds 2 and 3: What? What is it? *(They notice the angel and scream.)*

Angel: Do not be afraid.

Shepherd 2: Don't be afraid? Yeah, right.

Shepherd 3: Yeah, it's way too late for that.

Angel: Be QUIET! I bring you tidings of great joy.

Shepherd 1: Huh?

Angel: For to you this day in the city of David is born the Messiah. And you will find him wrapped in swaddling clothes and lying in a manager.

Shepherds *stare blankly at the angel.*

Angel: Just get out of here and go see the Messiah.

Shepherd 1: We can't leave the sheep.

Shepherd 2: Yeah, the owner told us if anything happened to a sheep and one of us wasn't dead, then we'd all be.

Angel: All right, I'll watch the sheep.

Shepherd 1: But what about the lions?

Shepherd 2: And tigers.

Shepherd 3: And bears.

Shepherds: Oh my.

Angel: Are you really so stupid as to think that a lion is going to mess with me?

Shepherd 2: [He or she] has a point.

Shepherd 3: Yes. And, really, I could use a night off.

Angel: GET OUT OF HERE!

Shepherds 1, 2, *and* **3** *begin walking off the stage.*

Shepherd 1: What city is the City of David?

Shepherd 2: I think Bethlehem is.

Shepherd 3: OK, so what are swaddling clothes?

All exit.

SCENE 12

Mary, *with the baby Jesus in her arms, and* **Joseph** *enter.*

Mary: Isn't he wonderful?

Notes

Joseph: Yes, and so are you.

Shepherds 1, 2, *and* **3** *enter.*

Shepherd 1: OK, this is the city of David.

Shepherd 2: But how many mangers do you think there are around her?

Shepherd 3: I still want to know what swaddling clothes are!

Joseph: Over here, guys.

Shepherd 1: Right.

Shepherd 2: Cute baby.

Shepherd 3: That's what swaddling clothes are? Why didn't the angel just say "diaper"?

Shepherd 1: Now what?

Shepherd 2: I don't know. The angel didn't say anything about what we are supposed to do.

Joseph: Angel?

Shepherd 2: Yeah. This angel showed up and told us to come here. We figured we'd better do it. I mean, [he or she] offered to watch our sheep. Can't go wrong there.

Joseph: Trust me, I understand the whole angel thing.

Shepherd 1: Should we go back to the sheep?

Shepherd 3: I don't want to go back there.

Shepherd 2: You know, the angel didn't give us a curfew or anything.

Shepherds: All right!

Shepherd 1: Let's rejoice . . .

Shepherd 2: . . . and give thanks . . .

Shepherd 3: . . . for the great things we've seen and heard!

The lights go down. No one exits.

SCENE 13

Enter **Youth Leader, Joseph, Mary** *carrying the the baby Jesus,* **Wise Person, Astrologer, King,** *and* **Camel.** *The lights go up.*

Youth Leader: A little over a year later.

King: Are we there yet?

Astrologer: Yes.

King: Really?

Astrologer: Yep.

King: Finally!

Wise Person: OK, now we fall down and worship him.

King, Astrologer, Wise Person, *and* **Camel** *kneel before the holy family.*

Shepherd 3: We didn't fall down and worship.

Shepherd 1: Think we should?

Shepherd 2: SHHHHH!

Astrologer: *(Getting up.)* Well, here's my gift. Time to go.

King: We just got here.

Wise Person: You know how long it took us to get here?

King: Yeah.

Wise Person: The ride home won't be any shorter. And we'll even have to take a different route.

King: Oh, yeah.

> **Wise Person, King, Astrologer,** *and* **Camel** *exit.*

Astrologer: *(From just off stage.)* Anyway, I really don't want to be here when they open the myrrh.

King: *(From just off stage.)* You said "ride home." Does that mean that I can ride [name of camel] home?

Camel: *(From just off stage.)* BWAW!

Shepherd 2: Yeah, that angel might be getting angry that we're still not back. I mean, it's been over a year.

Shepherd 3: And I miss the dog.

> **Shepherds 1, 2,** *and* **3** *exit.* **Angel** *enters.*

Angel: You didn't scream!

Mary: We're getting used to some pretty strange stuff.

Angel: OK! Joe, it's time that you and Mary left too. How would like to see the pyramids?

Joseph: Pyramids?

Angel: Yeah, things are going to be a little tense around here until Herod dies. And you two still haven't had a real honeymoon. Take a vacation; go to Egypt.

> **Mary, Joseph,** *and* **Donkey Front and Back** *exit.*

Angel: See you later. *(To the audience.)* Of course, this isn't the end of the story; it is only the beginning. But, it is the end of the play. Good night.

> **Angel** *exits.*

Service Project Ideas

A good way to prepare for the gift of Jesus Christ during Advent is to extend Christian love to others by giving them your time and energy. Here are some suggestions for Advent-season service projects:

✝ **Toy Collection.** Gather new toys to donate to a local toy drive for underprivileged children, or organize your own drive. You might collect toys after a Sunday service or in conjunction with a church Christmas program.

✝ **Adopt-a-Grandparent.** Collect the names of homebound congregation members or of local nursing- or retirement-home residents. Pair each participating youth with one of these persons for the duration of Advent. Encourage them to make cards, visit, call, and find other ways to brighten the season for their new friends.

✝ **Christmas Elves.** Create teams of youth and adults in your congregation who will volunteer to be "Christmas elves" and help clean the yard or home of an older adult or person in the church who has a disability. The teams could also help decorate the person's home for the season.

✝ **Remember Those in Service.** Collect the names of members or friends of your congregation serving in the military. Make Christmas cards, and send the cards to these persons. Also, consider hosting a Christmas party for the families or children of those who are away on military service.

✝ **Disaster Relief.** Organize a fundraiser for an international disaster relief, and have the event showcase your youth's gifts and talents. For example, you might host a Christmas concert to raise money or to collect supplies for a relief agency such as The United Methodist Committee on Relief (*www.umcor.org*).

✝ **Faith and Action.** Learn about an important issue for the poor and marginalized in your community. For example, a new waste dump might be planned to be established near a low-income neighborhood. Organize the youth to write letters to local, state, or federal officials in support of those at risk. Help the youth make the connection between their efforts and their faith.

✝ **A Day Off, a Day On.** Ask the teens to volunteer to give a church custodian (or another member of the church's service staff) a special paid day off by filling in at the church for him or her during the youth's school vacation. (If your congregation has only one part-time custodian, you might give him or her an entire week off.) Check with your church's pastor or administrator. This service could provide a hard-working person a needed to day to rest, be with family, or go Christmas shopping.

✝ **O Christmas Tree.** Purchase small, artificial Christmas trees. Have the youth decorate the trees and deliver them to homebound members or others who might not have a Christmas tree.

✝ **Remember Those in Prison.** With guidance from your pastor and appropriate authorities, allow your youth to visit prisoners at your county's jail. Have the youth make Christmas cards for the inmates. If visitation is not a possibility, ask the warden to distribute the cards to the jail's residents.

Worship Ideas

Have a Progressive Nativity*

Every week in Advent, add pieces of the Nativity a few at a time. Let the anticipation build as each piece finds its place around the manger. Talk about the symbols as they are placed in the worship space. Invite the youth to secretly move the pieces throughout your room as if the pieces are on a journey. This progression can be a fun way to excite the youth about the coming of the Christ Child.

Consider encouraging the youth to collect Nativity figurines from different cultures and art styles. Powerful symbolism builds when the figures around the manger are different colors, sizes, and shapes. Once all of the different pieces are around the manger, have a discussion about what it must be like in the kingdom of God when cultures and colors are not a mark of separation, but of unity as people of God.

*From *Worship Feast: 100 Awesome Ideas for Postmodern Youth*, page 40 (Abingdon Press, 2003; ISBN 0687063574).

Have an Owlah Service for New Year's Eve

Owlah is a Hebrew word meaning "burnt offering." Owlah services allow us to release our sins from the previous year—to let them go "up in smoke"—while recognizing that Christ has made atonement for all of our sins.

An Owlah service includes a litany built around the Ten Commandments, and a time of prayer and reflection, during which the participants confess their sins from the previous year by writing them on a notecard. These cards are collected in a basket, and the service ends with the burning of the confession cards in an outdoor fire.

For more information, see "Standing at the Door" from The General Board of Discipleship of The United Methodist Church (*www.gbod.org/worship/articles/standing_door/p52.html*).

Learn New Songs and Hymns

Your hymnal or songbook of preference probably includes several well-known Christmas hymns and carols, such as "Silent Night," "Away in a Manger," and "Joy to the World." Chances are it also includes many seasonal hymns and songs your group has not sung before.

Challenge your teens during this year's Advent and Christmas worship services by incorporating hymns and songs that are unfamiliar to your group. Consider trying your hand at some songs from cultural traditions other than your own.

Have a Las Posadas Christmas Party

Las Posadas is a Mexican tradition recalling Mary and Joseph's struggle to find shelter on the night of Jesus' birth. A traditional Las Posadas celebration takes place over eight nights at eight different homes, but you may celebrate Las Posadas on one night at one setting.

First, prepare a Christmas party complete with food and games; if you can, have it at someone's house. Arrange for all partygoers (aside from the hosts) to arrive at the house together, and instruct someone to bring along a baby doll (which will represent the Christ Child). When the visitors arrive, the host will at first not allow them to enter. However, after a series of Scripture readings and responses, the host will invite everyone inside for the celebration.

See the sample Los Posadas service on the following page.

Worship Ideas
(Continued)

A Sample Las Posadas Service*

Beforehand, select a family to host and prepare the celebration. (You might ask different youth to provide certain foods or party supplies, but the host family should be responsible for decorating the party area and setting out the food.) At an appointed time, the participants should arrive at the hosts' house.

Each person should have a Bible or a printed page featuring the Scriptures below. Traditionally, the participants carry lighted candles and sing as they walk toward the host home. You might assign one volunteer to play the role of Mary and another to be Joseph. Other participants may dress as shepherds, magi, sheep, or donkeys.

One of the guests, standing outside the house, begins the service by knocking on the door and reading aloud Revelation 3:20.

The guests then say:
Will you give us a place to stay?
We are pilgrims who have come all the way from Nazareth, and we are tired from our journey.
My name is Joseph; I am a carpenter.
My wife's name is Mary. She is pregnant and can travel no longer.
I beg you, please give us a place to stay.

The hosts respond:
Even though you say you are tired from your journey, we do not open our door to strangers.
We don't care who you are or where you have come from; just let us sleep.

The guests then read aloud John 1:10-12 ("to all who received him . . . he gave power to become children of God") in unison.

The hosts respond:
Who are God's children?

The guests then read aloud Romans 8:14 ("all who are led by the Spirit of God are children of God") in unison.

The hosts respond:
What does the Spirit of God want us to do?

The guests then read aloud Matthew 22:37, 39 (the two greatest commandments) followed by Galatians 5:22-23a (the "fruit of the Spirit").

The hosts respond:
How do we know if we truly love God and have faith?

The guests then read aloud James 2:14-17 ("faith, by itself, if it has no works, is dead").

The hosts then open the door and switch on the lights inside the house.

The hosts then say:
We would be happy to give you a place to stay.
Come in, Mary and Joseph.
We welcome you into our home, but, more importantly, we welcome you into our hearts.

The hosts then pray:
Almighty God,
    help us to rid ourselves of evil and wickedness,
and fill us with the light of your Son, Jesus Christ.
Thank you for sending Jesus to live as one of us,
    to show us how to live, and to redeem us,
so that when he returns in glory,
we will have eternal life through Christ,
who lives and reigns with you and your Holy Spirit,
now and forever. Amen.

*Adapted from "Las Posadas (Service of Shelter for the Holy Family)," from *The United Methodist Book of Worship*. Adapted and translated. Copyright © 1992 by The United Methodist Publishing House; pages 266–268. Used by permission.

Christmas Celebration Ideas

Advent and Christmas are important seasons of the Christian year that invite reverence and reflection. But because of God's gift of Jesus Christ, Christians also have a big reason to be joyful and to celebrate. Below are some ideas for planning a Christmas party to recognize both the work of preparation undertaken during Advent and the humble, glorious birth of Jesus Christ.

Getting Into the Party

Two or three weeks before your Christmas party, send out invitations and make announcements in your church bulletin, newsletter, e-mail list, or website.

If you wish, charge an admission fee to your party. Make the fee something that benefits those in need (but do not keep out any youth who forget to bring something). Ideas for fees are:

✝ a canned food for the local food pantry

✝ a Christmas card to be sent to a homebound member of your congregation

✝ a new item of children's clothing for a local clothes closet or an underprivileged family your church or group has adopted for Christmas

Breaking the Ice

As your partygoers gather, play some seasonal music and invite them to have some refreshments.

Engage the youth in a simple game or activity as they arrive. You might create a Christmas word search, do an activity from one of the programs in this book, or set up a station where the teens can create or decorate Christmas cards for homebound church members.

When everyone has arrived, play a game that requires discussion and interaction. For example:

✝ Give each youth a pencil and a sheet of paper. Instruct the teens to quickly interview a designated number of other youth and to record each youth's name and one of his or her family's Christmas traditions. Each interviewee must initial the interviewer's paper.

✝ Gather the students in a circle. Ask a volunteer to name a gift he or she would like to receive for Christmas that begins with the same letter as his or her first name. For example, someone named Morgan might say, "I'd like an MP3 player," and someone named Whitney might say, "I'd like world peace." The second person must say the first person's name and desired gift along with the second person's first name and gift. Continue until you have gone around the entire circle and the last person has recited everyone's name and desired gift.

Share a Meal

Consider having a group meal as a part of your celebration. Begin by offering a prayer of thanksgiving and blessing, such as the following:

> Lord Jesus, Light of the World, your birth means that God's people need not be in darkness. Your arrival means that no one need be hungry. Your presence means that no one need be lonely. Bless our fellowship now and the meal we share. And strengthen us to nourish the world for which you were born. Amen.

Some Christmas Fun

Enjoy your time together with some Christmas activities, games, stories, or movies. Here are some ideas:

Decorate a chrismon tree. Have the youth create simple Christian symbols and use them as ornaments on a small Christmas tree. (For a list of chrismons and their meanings, visit *www.why christmas.com/customs/customs_chrismons.html*.)

Christmas Celebration Ideas
(Continued)

Create a living nativity. Select volunteers to portray each of the characters in the Christmas story from Luke 2:1-20 (which does not mention Magi or wisemen). Read aloud Luke 2:1-20, and invite volunteers to act out the story. You or a youth volunteer should be the narrator, and the characters should read their speaking parts. To make the experience more realistic, arrange to do your living nativity outside a hotel or at a stable.

Make some music. Have musicians (including some of the youth) play instruments such as guitar and piano and lead the group in singing some familiar Christmas hymns and songs. Invite the teens to learn some new Christmas hymns.

Go caroling. Stop by homes near your church, neighborhoods where church members live, or a retirement community or nursing home.

Have a candy-cane relay race.

a. Divide the group into two or more teams so that no more than ten youth are on a team. Instruct the teams to stand in single-file lines behind a starting line.

b. Mark a finish line fifteen to twenty feet away from the starting line.

c. Give each person a candy cane.

d. The first two persons in each line must hook their candy canes together and move to the finish line as quickly as possible without their candy canes coming unhooked. (If the canes unhook, both persons must return to the starting line and try again.)

e. The first person stays at the finish line while the second person runs back to the starting line and hooks his or her candy cane with the next person's candy cane. These two youth then dash to the finish line with their candy canes linked. This process continues until all team members reach the finish line. The first team to have all of its members at the finish line wins.

Write letters or Christmas cards. Address them to persons from your church or community who are serving in the military or to missionaries whom your church or denomination supports.

Play Christmas charades. Divide the youth into teams, or choose volunteers who will silently act out clues to help the group guess these and other Christmas-related items: an angel, a manger, Mary, a star, a Christmas tree, Jesus, no room in the inn, and Bethlehem. To challenge the teens, throw in King Herod, the angel Gabriel, Anna, or Simeon. If you divide the youth into teams, award the teams one point for each item guessed correctly.

Go Forth, and Celebrate Christ's Coming

Close your Christmas party with a group prayer. Invite each person to pray for the church, your community, and the world. Ask God to grant every person a special Christmas blessing.

Give each partygoer a small bag of Christmas treats as he or she leaves.

Other Christmas party ideas can be found in *Holidays, Holy Days, and Other Big Days for Youth,* by Todd Outcalt (Abingdon Press, 1999; ISBN 0687082048).

New Year's Celebration Ideas

People rarely think of New Year's Eve and Day as Christian holidays. But the church has long seen them as appropriate times to celebrate, reflect, pray, give thanks, and rejoice. Here are some ideas for giving your teens a safe, fun, and meaningful way to welcome the new year:

Getting Into the Party

Two or three weeks prior to your New Year's Eve party, send out invitations and make announcements in your church bulletin, newsletter, e-mail list, or website.

To emphasize the theme of newness, require everyone to wear at least one "new" thing. It does not have to be something significant. The youth might, for example, just wear something they got for Christmas. Have a box of cheap and silly "new" things on hand for those who do not have on something new. (These items could include cheap beads, an ugly tie, and so forth.)

Breaking the Ice

As your partygoers gather, play some seasonal music and invite them to have some refreshments.

Engage the youth in a simple game or activity. Here are two possibilities:

Candy-Loop Race: Many people celebrate New Year's with a kiss. Doing so would probably not be appropriate in your setting, but you can help the group get close and have fun by having a candy-loop race.

✚ Divide the group into teams so that no more than ten persons are on a team. Instruct each team to form a single file line.

✚ Give each team a roll of candies with a hole in them (such as Lifesavers®), and give each individual a toothpick.

✚ The first person in each line will hold her or his toothpick in her or his teeth then place a candy loop on the toothpick.

✚ Using only their toothpicks held in their teeth, each team must pass a candy loop from the front to the back of the line.

✚ You may have the teams race to see which team can pass one candy loop from the front to the back of the line in the least amount of time, or you may have them compete to see which team can pass the most candies from the front to the back of the line in a specified amount of time.

New Year's Limericks. Have each person write a New Year's limerick using his or her name. For example:

> There's a guy whom we all know as Bryan
> Who just wished that he could be a flyin'
> Flapped his arms like finch
> Left the ground not an inch
> So, this new year he'll just stop a tryin'

Share a Meal or Snack

Consider having a meal or snack as a part of your party. Begin by offering a prayer of blessing and thanksgiving for the coming year, such as:

Eternal God, maker of time and space, giver of all good and perfect gifts, we thank you for the year that has just passed and the year that lies ahead. Forgive us for the ways we have failed you in the past year, and look on us with mercy in the new year. Grant that we may live each new day with hearts thankful for your love and grace. Let this meal strengthen us for the days ahead, that we may fill them with joyful service to you and our neighbors. In the name of Jesus Christ our Lord, Amen.

New Year's Celebration Ideas

(Continued)

Some New Year's Fun

Enjoy your time together with some New-Year's-themed activities or games. Here are some ideas:

Renew your commitment. Begin the new year with a renewal of commitment to Jesus Christ. For example, you might use the Covenant Renewal Service from *The United Methodist Book of Worship* (copyright © 1992 by The United Methodist Publishing House; page 288).

Read aloud Revelation 21:1-5. In this Scripture God makes all things new. Too often we focus on what God *has* done without recognizing what God *is doing* or *will do* in the future. Lead the youth in a discussion about how God is at work now and what God might do in the new year.

Begin the New Year with a toast. You don't need champagne and wine glasses to wish the best to your friends in the new year. A toast is just as effective with soda and plastic cups. Ask for volunteers to write toasts for the party. Allow each volunteer time to propose a toast.

Play Last Year's Charades. Divide the students into two teams. Alternating the teams, have each youth one at a time silently act out for his or her team a movie or a news or sports story from the previous year. Award a team a point for guessing in a specified amount of time (such as one or two minutes) what its member is acting out.

Play New Year's Memory.

a. You will need twenty pairs of index cards.

b. On each pair of cards, write either a memory from the past year related to your youth ministry or something big your youth might have planned for the coming year (such as "beach retreat" or "mission trip").

c. Shuffle all of the cards, and arrange them in eight rows of five cards each.

d. Divide the group into teams of two or three. Then have the teams take turns turning over two cards to find a match. If a team finds a match, award that team one point and remove that pair of cards. If not, turn the cards back over. The teams will succeed if the team members help one another remember where certain cards are located.

f. The team with the most pairs of cards wins.

Play Pin-the-New-Year-on-the-Calendar. On a large sheet of paper, create a calendar of December and January, but leave blank space where January 1 should be. Cut out several pieces of paper the size of the blank space, and label them "January 1: New Year's Day." (You might decorate them with pictures of party hats or firecrackers.) One at a time, blindfold the youth and challenge them to tape January 1 as close as possible to the missing space on the calendar.

Ring in the New Year!

If your party is going until the new year begins, hand out noisemakers and streamers. Find a TV or radio station or a webcast covering the New Year's celebration, and start the countdown.

Have everyone form a circle and hold hands, and spend the last ten seconds of the old year and the first ten seconds of the new year praying for one another, your church, and the world. Then exchange signs of peace and love.

Other New Year's party ideas can be found in *Holidays, Holy Days, and Other Big Days for Youth,* by Todd Outcalt (Abingdon Press, 1999; ISBN 0687082048).

Bible Dictionary

Advent: the first season of the Christian year. Including the four Sundays prior to Christmas Day, Advent is traditionally a time for repentance and preparation for celebrating the birth of Jesus Christ. The church has long used purple as the chief color for Advent, since purple is associated with both repentance and the royalty of the expected King. Some churches use blue as a royal Advent color because blue is a church color associated with hope and because purple is also used during Lent.

Advent wreath: a symbol of the Advent season, composed of a circular wreath (which is often evergreen branches) and four purple candles arranged at twelve, three, six, and nine o'clock, respectively. Each week of Advent, one of the candles is lighted until all four are lit, representing the approach of the birth of Jesus, the light of the world. Some churches substitute a pink candle (symbolizing joy) for the third Sunday of Advent, as a break from the repentant symbolism of the purple candles. Often a large white candle called the Christ candle is located at the center of the wreath but is not lit until Christmas Eve or Christmas Day.

Angels: those who, in the Bible, serve as direct messengers from God. Their name comes from the Greek word *angelos,* meaning "messenger." Scripture does not describe angels' appearance in detail but instead emphasizes what they say. Only two angels are mentioned by name in the Protestant Scriptures: Gabriel (Daniel 8:15-26; 9:21-27; Luke 1:11-20, 26-38) and Michael (Daniel 10:13, 21; 12:1; Jude 9; Revelation 12:7). (Additional angels are named in books that are included in the Roman Catholic and Orthodox Old Testaments—books Protestants refer to as the Apocrypha.)

Anna: a Jewish prophet who appears in Luke 2:36-38, when the infant Jesus ias presented in the Temple in Jerusalem. Luke describes Anna as a faithful widow who devoted herself completely to prayer and worship of God. She speaks prophetically about Jesus' role in redeeming Israel. There is no record of Anna outside Luke's Gospel.

Baptism: an ancient religious symbol or rite involving ritual washing. Baptism appears in the Gospels first with John the Baptist baptizing his followers in the wilderness as a symbol of their repentance, or willingness to turn back to God. In the synoptic Gospels (Matthew, Mark, and Luke), John baptized Jesus; according to Matthew and Mark, Jesus was baptized in the Jordan River. Jesus mentioned baptism as a practice that united him and his followers (Mark 10:39-40).

Baptism became the primary Christian sacrament of conversion and entry into the church, and the Acts of the Apostles and Paul's epistles mention the rite several times. It represents God's gracious acceptance of humanity as well as Christians' commitment to live as disciples of Jesus Christ.

Bethlehem: a city in Israel located about five miles south of Jerusalem. In the Old Testament, Bethlehem figured into the story of the Levite's concubine in Judges 19 and, more importantly, was the hometown of Naomi in the Book of Ruth. Ruth moved to Bethlehem with Naomi (Ruth 1:22), and the small town became the home of Ruth's great-grandson, King David.

Of course, Bethlehem is best known as the site of Jesus' birth (Matthew 2:1, 5-6; Luke 2:1-7; John 7:42). The Gospel of Luke says that Joseph and Mary were summoned to Bethlehem, Joseph's ancestral home, because a Roman governmental census had required all to go "to their own towns to be registered" (Luke 2:3). Matthew claims that Jesus' birth in Bethlehem fulfilled a prophecy from Micah 5:2 about a ruler from Bethlehem who was to rule Israel. Jesus' birth in Bethlehem connected him with the lineage and story of King David, one of the most famous and honored rulers in the Israelite history.

Census (or enrollment): a governmental project in which all of the residents of a particular area or region are registered and counted, often for purposes of taxation or conscription into military service. The Old Testament mentions such enrollments. (See, for example, Numbers 1:1-49; 2 Samuel 24:1-9; and Ezra 2:2b-67).

The best-known biblical census is the Roman census in Luke's Gospel, an order that required Mary and Joseph to go to Bethlehem to register. Luke says the census took place "while Quirinius was governor of Syria" (Luke 2:2b). This statement poses a problem for scholars, since Quirinius did not become governor of Syria until more than a decade after the assumed date of Jesus' birth (6 B.C.). Jesus was born during the reign of Herod the Great, but Quirinius did not assume the office of governor until after Herod's death. Some people have suggested that Quirinius held a different government job at the time and was named in the story of the enrollment because he would have been familiar to Luke's readers.

Chrismon: an abbreviation for the term *Christ monogram*. A Chrismon can be one of a variety of Christian symbols that represent the person, life, or story of Jesus Christ. Most properly, a Chrismon incorporates letters of Jesus' name; an example is the Chi-Rho symbol, which consists of the Greek letters Chi (X) and Rho (P) superimposed together. Many churches decorate an evergreen tree with Chrismons as part of Advent and Christmas celebrations. The idea of a Chrismon tree first came to fruition at Ascension Lutheran Church in Danville, Virginia in 1957.

Elizabeth: the mother of John the Baptist, wife of Zechariah, and relative of Mary the mother of Jesus. (Elizabeth's exact relationship to Mary is unknown.) Elizabeth was past the normal childbearing age when John was conceived and born. Mary visited Elizabeth when they were each pregnant with their respective sons; during this visit John famously jumped in his mother's womb (Luke 1:44).

Gabriel: an angelic messenger sent by God to announce the impending birth of John to Zechariah and Elizabeth and then to tell Mary of Jesus' conception and expected birth. Gabriel appears in the Old Testament in Daniel 8:15-26; 9:21-27. Ancient Jewish and Christian tradition considered Gabriel one of the four archangels, and he appears in ancient extrabiblical writings such as 1 Enoch.

John the Baptist: a contemporary and, according to Luke, relative of Jesus. John's ministry involved calling people back to God through repentance and baptism. All four Gospels suggest that John's ministry was a precursor to Jesus' ministry. In Matthew, Mark, and Luke, John baptized Jesus; in Matthew and Mark, he proclaimed Jesus as the one who would come with the power of God to baptize "with the Holy Spirit and fire" (Matthew 3:11b). The Book of Acts suggests that some of John's disciples, namely Priscilla and Aquila, were also received into the early church (18:24-28; 19:1-7).

John was imprisoned and put to death at the command of King Herod Antipas (Matthew 14:1-12; Mark 6:14-29; Luke 9:7-9). The Gospels report that John's death was a favor from Herod to Herodias—Herod's niece and wife and former wife of Herod's brother Philip—and that John was beheaded. (Herodias had requested John's head on a platter.) John had condemned the marriage of Herod and Herodias as unlawful (Matthew 14:3-4). According to the Jewish historian Josephus, Herod executed John at the fortress of Machaerus.

Joseph: a man who, according to the Gospel of Matthew, was a descendant of King David and was engaged to become the husband of a young woman named Mary. Little is mentioned of this man chosen to raise Jesus as a human father, but Joseph does serve as an example one who faithfully trusted God and acted upon God's instructions. Matthew 13:55 suggests that Joseph was a carpenter or skilled artisan of some sort.

King Herod the Great: a Jewish king who ruled in the region of Palestine as a puppet governor under the rule of the Romans from

40–4 B.C. Herod ruled at the time of Jesus' birth (which is assumed to be 6 B.C.) but died shortly thereafter. He is notorious for the massacre of the infants. Though this episode is not mentioned outside Matthew's Gospel, other historical sources attest to Herod's ruthlessness. Following his death, his kingdom was divided among his three sons, Archelaus, Herod Antipas (often referred to in the Gospels simply as "Herod"), and Philip.

Mary, the Mother of Jesus: a young Hebrew woman chosen by God to conceive and bear Jesus. At the time she conceived Jesus, the Gospels report that she was a virgin engaged to a man named Joseph. Unlike Joseph, Mary is prominent in all four Gospel accounts, though she is never named in John. Mark suggests that Mary gave birth to several other children (Mark 6:3).

Some scholars feel that Mark portrays Jesus' relationship with his mother in a negative light. (See Mark 3:31-35; 6:2-4.) Matthew and Luke give a more favorable impression of Jesus and Mary's relationship. John's Gospel alone includes a story of Mary at her son's crucifixion. Jesus (from the cross) instructs "the disciple whom Jesus loved" (whom we presume is John) to care for his mother (John 19:26-27).

Shepherds: people who look after flocks of sheep, goats, or both. In the Gospel of Luke, shepherds working in the fields were among the first to receive news from hosts of angels that Jesus had been born. Since sheep were so important to Jewish and Israelite religious life and to the local economy, shepherding was a common occupation. Socially and economically, shepherds ranked among the lowest in society, though many biblical heroes (such as Abraham, Moses, and David) worked as shepherds. The shepherds' being the first to learn of Jesus' birth suggests that the good news of Christ is meant for all people, regardless of social status.

Shepherd imagery is found throughout the Bible. In the Old Testament, references to shepherds are used in a variety of ways. (See, for example, Genesis 48:15; Psalm 23; Isaiah 44:28; Jeremiah 10:21; and Zechariah 11:4-17.) In the New Testament, Jesus is often compared to a shepherd; he famously refers to himself as the Good Shepherd in John 10:1-21. (See also Matthew 18:12-14; Hebrews 13:20; and 1 Peter 2:25.)

Simeon: a righteous and devout man who appears in Luke 2:25-35. The Holy Spirit guided Simeon to find the infant Jesus in the Temple in Jerusalem. Simeon praised God and pronounced that Jesus was the fulfillment of God's restoration of Israel's independence. He also cites the prophet Isaiah and proclaims that Jesus would be "a light for revelation to the Gentiles" (Luke 2:32) in addition to bringing glory to the Jews.

The Temple in Jerusalem: the center of Jewish worship in Jerusalem. In Luke 2:22-38, Jesus was presented as an infant to be dedicated to God in accordance with Levitical law. The Jerusalem Temple in Jesus' day (known by scholars as the Second Temple) was built under Ezra and Nehemiah in the sixth century B.C. following the Exile in Babylon. (See Ezra 3; Nehemiah 3.) The Roman army destroyed this temple in A.D. 70 after the Jewish revolt against Roman imperial rule. All that remains of the Temple is the Western Wall, or "Wailing Wall," which is a popular pilgrimage site for Jews today.

The Virgin Birth: the theological belief or doctrine that Jesus was conceived by and born of a woman who had not had sexual relations with a man (Matthew 1:18-25; Luke 1:26-38). While this doctrine is sometimes used to connote special status of Mary, it better conveys the truth of Jesus' special and unique nature as God's son.

Zechariah: a Hebrew priest, husband to Elizabeth, and father of John the Baptist. While serving his religious duties, Zechariah saw the angel Gabriel, who announced that Zechariah and his wife would have a son to be named John. Zechariah disbelieved Gabriel's words and was rendered unable to speak until after John was born.